KT-474-940

CHARTRES CATHEDRAL

Malcolm Miller

Photographs by Sonia Halliday
and Laura Lushington

First Edition 1985
Second Edition 1996

Copyright © Pitkin Guides Ltd 1996
Text copyright © Malcolm Miller 1980,
1985 and 1996
Photographs copyright © Sonia Halliday
and Laura Lushington, using Pentax 6 × 7
equipment.
Cover photograph by Sonia Halliday and
Mark Nicholson. Photography: pp 8 bottom,
11 top by Mark Nicholson; pp 42/43 by
Martin Marix Evans; pp 82/83 by Sonia
Halliday and Mark Nicholson.
Black-and-white illustrations by
John Fuller.
Illustration on pp 4/5 is based on original
artwork from *Stained Glass* by Lawrence
Lee, George Seddon & Francis Stephens,
photography by Sonia Halliday and Laura
Lushington, published by Mitchell Beazley.
Illustration on p 20 is reproduced from
The World Atlas of Architecture, foreword
by John Julius Norwich, published by
Mitchell Beazley.
Edited by Martin Marix Evans, Book
Packaging and Marketing.
Designed by Adrian Hodgkins Design.
Plans by John Buckley.

All rights reserved. No part of this book may
be reproduced or transmitted in any form or
by any means, electronic or mechanical,
including photocopying, recording or any
information storage and retrieval system,
without permission in writing from the
Publisher.

British Library Cataloguing in Publication
Data. A catalogue record for this book is
available from the British Library.

Published by PITKIN GUIDES,
Healey House, Dene Road, Andover,
Hampshire SP10 2AA, UK
Printed and bound in Great Britain.

ISBN 0 85372 737 6 English hardcover
edition
ISBN 0 85372 792 9 English paperback
edition

PREVIOUS PAGE: *The*
creation of Adam, on the
left, and Eve, on the
right, and the warning,
above, not to eat of the
fruit of the knowledge of
Good and Evil. Detail
from the Good Samaritan
window.

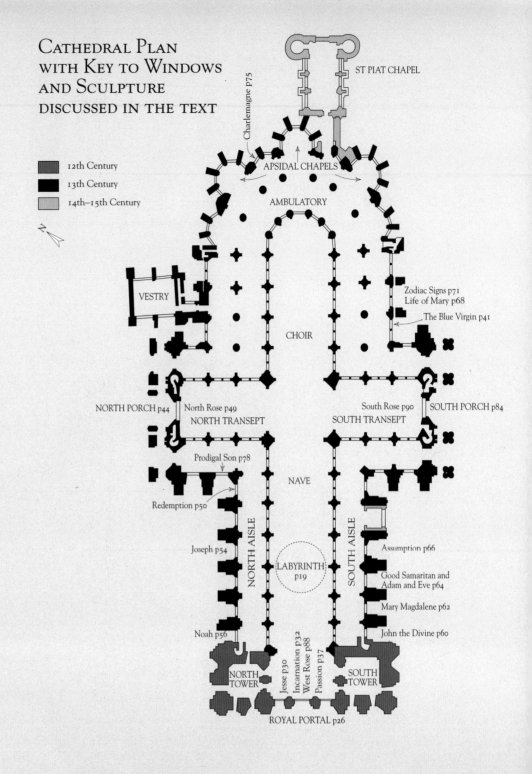

CATHEDRAL PLAN
WITH KEY TO WINDOWS
AND SCULPTURE
DISCUSSED IN THE TEXT

12th Century
13th Century
14th–15th Century

ST PIAT CHAPEL

Charlemagne p75

APSIDAL CHAPELS

AMBULATORY

VESTRY

Zodiac Signs p71
Life of Mary p68
The Blue Virgin p41

CHOIR

NORTH PORCH p44
North Rose p49
NORTH TRANSEPT

South Rose p90
SOUTH TRANSEPT
SOUTH PORCH p84

Prodigal Son p78

NAVE

Redemption p50

Joseph p54

NORTH AISLE

LABYRINTH
p19

SOUTH AISLE

Assumption p66

Good Samaritan and
Adam and Eve p64

Mary Magdalene p62

Noah p56

John the Divine p60

NORTH
TOWER

Jesse p30
Incarnation p32
West Rose p88
Passion p37

SOUTH
TOWER

ROYAL PORTAL p26

CONTENTS

References in the text to the numbers
on this plan are given in bold type.

THE NAVE – NORTH AISLE
Upper windows
155 St Martin 13th c. given by Citizens of Tours
156 St Martin and donors 13th and 19th c.
157 Mary and donors kneeling 13th c.
158 Abraham and Isaac 13th c.
159 Jesus. Sacrifice of Isaac 13th c.
160 Ploughmen donors 13th c.
161 St George, his martyrdom 13th c.
162 St Giles 13th c.
163 St George, killing dragon 13th c.
164 Apostle 13th c. Bankers donors.
165 Six apostles
166 Mary, *sedes sapientiae*; Jesus in her womb.
    Doves symbolize other six gifts of Holy Spirit
167 St Nicholas 13th c.
168 Four apostles 13th c. Furriers donors.
169 St Thomas of Canterbury 13th c.
170 St Stephen 13th c.
171 St Lawrence 13th c.
172 Bishop Lubin of Chartres 13th c.
173 Prophets: Jonah, Daniel, Habakkuk
174 The three temptations of Christ
175 A bishop (inscription lost) 13th c.

THE NAVE – NORTH AISLE
Lower windows
59 Symbolic window of the Redemption 13th
   and 19th c.
60 St Nicholas 13th c.
61 Joseph 13th c.
62 St Eustace 13th c.
63 St Lubin 13th c.
64 Noah 13th c.

THE WEST ROSE AND LANCET WINDOWS
1 Jesse Tree 12th c.
2 Incarnation 12th c.
3 Passion and Resurrection 12th c.
176 West Rose
    The Last Judgement c.1215

THE NAVE – SOUTH AISLE
Upper windows
65 Mary the Egyptian
66 St Laumer 13th c.
67 An abbot 13th c.
68 St James the Greater 13th c.
69 St Peter 13th c.
70 Christ between alpha and omega 13th c.
71 Mary suckling, and a *Noli me tangere* 13th c.
72 St Foy 13th c.
73 St Solemnis (5th c. bishop of Chartres)
74 St James the Greater 13th c.
75 St Philip and Jeremiah 13th c.
76 St Jerome 13th c.
77 St Caletric 13th c.
78 St Bartholomew and Moses, hidden by organ
79 St Augustine 13th c.
80 & 81 Walled in, date unknown
82 St Gregory the Great 13th c.
83 Two saintly women
84 St Symphorian, mostly 19th c.
85 St Hilary 13th c.

THE NAVE – SOUTH AISLE
Lower windows
4 St John the Divine 13th c.
5 Mary Magdalene 13th c.
6 Parable of the Good Samaritan 13th c.
7 Assumption 13th c.
8 Vendôme Chapel window 15th c.
9 Miracles of Mary 13th and 20th c.

THE NORTH TRANSEPT
Lower windows
56 The Peace window, given by German Friends
   of Chartres 1971
57 St Lawrence (destroyed in 1791, except border.
   Modern glass 1967)
58 Parable of the Prodigal Son 13th c.

THE NORTH TRANSEPT
Upper windows
136 Annunciation and Nativity and Adoration of
    Magi 13th c.
137 St Eustace 13th c.
138 & 144 Christ blessing 13th c.
    (NB 2 windows same)
139 St Philip and St Jude 13th c.
140 St Andrew and St Philip
141 A priest donor
142 St Thomas and St Jude 13th c.

THE SOUTH TRANSEPT
Lower windows
10 St Apollinaris 13th c. and grisaille 1328
11 Destroyed 1791
12 St Fulbert, 1954. Given by American
   Architects' Association.

THE SOUTH TRANSEPT
Upper windows
86 St Peter 13th c.
87 St Paul 13th c.
88 Jean de Courville donor 13th c.
89 St Anthony 13th c.
90 20th c. window
91 A priest donor
92 Micah
93 Malachi
94 Pierre Mauclerc donor

143 St Thomas and St Barnaby 13th c.
145 North Rose window c.1230 and 5 lancets
146, 147, 148 Grisaille 13th c. (with fleur-de-lis
    and castles as beneath rose)
149 Anne and Joachim 19th c. (original destroyed
    in 1791)
150 Annunciation and Visitation 13th c.
151 St Anne with Mary 19th c.
152 Annunciation to Shepherds and Presentation
    at Temple 13th c.
153 Death and Assumption of Mary 13th c.
154 Count of Boulogne, Philip Boarskin donor
    13th c.

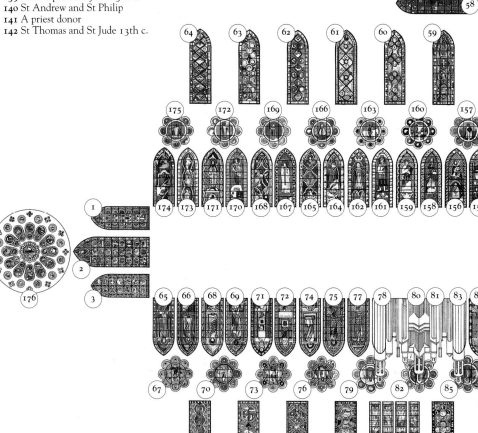

95 South Rose window and lancets c.1225
96 Hosea 13th c.
97 A prophet. Pierre Mauclerc donor
98 & 101 Virgin and Child 13th c.
99 St Come and St Damian 13th c.
100 St Gervais and St Protais 13th c.
102 St Denis and Clement family donors 13th c.
103 Two saints 13th c.
104 John the Baptist 13th c.

THE AMBULATORY

Upper windows

105 Nativity and Flight into Egypt, and Colinus, donor, playing chess

106 St John the Divine and St James the Greater and Adoration of Magi 13th c.

107 Beaumont donor 13th c.
108, 109 Removed 1788
110 Courtenay donor 13th c.
111 St Paul 13th c.
112 St Vincent
113 & 116 Montfort donor 13th c.
114, 115, 124, 125, 130
　13th c. glass destroyed in 18th c.
117 Annunciation to Zacharias and John the Baptist and Baptism of Jesus 13th c. Bankers donors
118 Daniel, Jeremiah and Cherub. Drapers donors

119 Moses with burning bush and Isaiah and Angel 13th c. Bakers donors
120 Annunciation and Visitation and Mary *sedes sapientiae* 13th c. Bakers donors
121 Aaron and Angel 13th c.
122 David and Ezekiel and Cherub 13th c. Butchers donors
123 Peter leaves prison, meets Jesus 13th c. Bankers donors
126 Louis VIII as Dauphin 13th c.
127, 128 St Martin
129 Count Thibault VI of Chartres
131 Grisaille 20th c.
132 King Ferdinand of Castile 13th c.
133 Two groups of pilgrims 13th c.
134 Virgin and Child 13th c.
135 Jesus seated between candlesticks

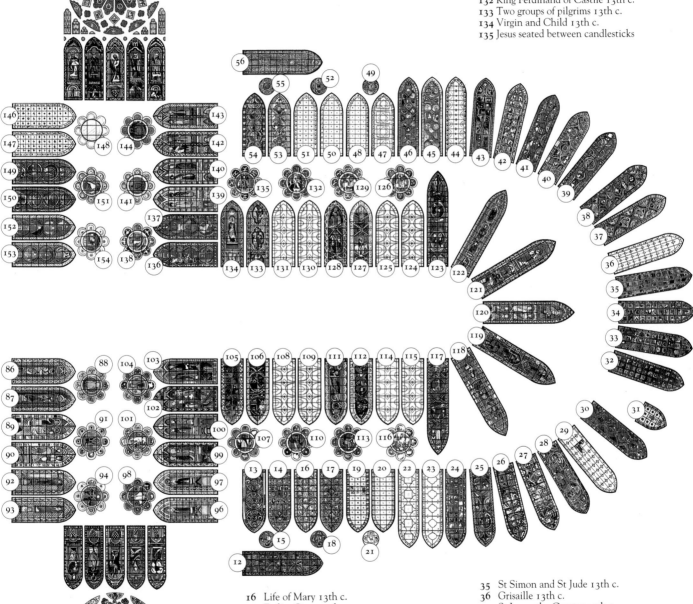

THE AMBULATORY

Lower windows

13 St Anthony and St Paul Anchorite
14 Temptations of Jesus
　Marriage feast of Cana
　Blue Virgin 12th c.
15 Virgin and Child

16 Life of Mary 13th c.
17 Zodiac Signs 13th c.
18 Crucifixion 13th c.
19, 20, 21 Grisaille 14th c. and Annunciation
22 & 23 Grisaille 17th c.
24 St Martin 13th c.
25 St Thomas Becket 13th c.
26 St Margaret and St Catherine 13th c.
27 St Nicholas 13th and 20th c.
28 St Remy 13th c.
29 Grisaille 13th c. and St Nicholas 15th c.
30 St Sylvester 13th c.
31 Grisaille St Piat 14th c.
32 St Paul 13th and 19th c.
33 St Andrew 13th and 19th c.
34 Apostles 13th and 19th c.

35 St Simon and St Jude 13th c.
36 Grisaille 13th c.
37 St James the Greater 13th c.
38 Charlemagne 13th c.
39 St Theodore and St Vincent 13th c.
40 St Pantaleon 13th c.
41 St Stephen 13th c.
42 St Cheron 13th c.
43 St Savinian and St Potentian 13th c.
44 Grisaille 13th c.
45 St Julian the Hospitaler 13th c.
46 St Thomas 13th c.
47, 48, 50, 51 Grisaille 13th c.
49, 52, 55 Apocalyptic Christs 13th c.
　(3 rose windows)
53 St Nicholas 13th c.
54 St Germain of Auxerre 13th c.

THE HISTORY OF
CHARTRES CATHEDRAL

Chartres from Roman Times until 1194

The origins of Chartres are lost in the mists of time, where legend and history are interwoven, and have been further confused by the imagination of later centuries which mingled a Druidic tradition with a pre-Christian virgin-mother cult, first mentioned in the 14th century. In fact, although Gallo-Roman Chartres (Autricum), built on the river Eure (Autura), was already an oppidum of some importance, with an amphitheatre and two aqueducts, nothing whatsoever is known of either its religious life or its evangelization by the first Christians, which probably occurred during the early 4th century. Amongst the first bishops of Chartres are St Adventinus, who lived in the mid-4th century, and a St Martin, followed by Solemnis, who, according to the chronicle *De vita sancti Deodati*, helped to instruct Clovis I in the Christian faith in the late 5th century. Solemnis's successor, Bishop Adventinus II, attended the first Council of Orleans in 511 and another bishop of Chartres, St Lubin, went to both the fifth Council of Orleans in 550 and that of Paris five years later.

From the existence of these early bishops it may be deduced that there was at least one and probably several primitive cathedrals at Chartres before the first reference to the destruction of one, in 743, when Hunald, Duke of Aquitaine, having quarrelled with Charles Martel's sons, sacked Chartres.

LEFT: *The north gallery of Fulbert's immense early 11th-century crypt, with barrel and groin vaults. The wooden statue over the altar is modern but is a copy of a carving known as Our Lady of the Crypt, probably made in the 12th century and burnt by revolutionaries in 1793.*

PREVIOUS PAGE: *A team of masons, donors of the St Chéron window, sculpting royal figures. Some of their tools and the wooden templates from which they worked can be seen hanging beneath the cusped arches.*

ABOVE: *An aerial view of the excavations (1990–92) in front of the cathedral. Part of a large 1st-century Roman public building was unearthed.*

ABOVE LEFT: *The Sancta Camisia, given to Chartres in 876 by King Charles the Bald and thought to have been worn by Mary when she gave birth to Christ. It is now displayed permanently in the northeast apsidal chapel and is in a modern reliquary.*

A few years later, one of Martel's sons, Pepin the Short (751–68), in a royal decree mentions gifts to the 'Church of Saint Mary' at Chartres, which is evidence that cathedrals at Chartres have been dedicated to Mary at least since Carolingian times. Hence, in the following century, when the city had been pillaged and its cathedral burnt by Vikings in 858, Charlemagne's grandson, Charles the Bald, presented the new church, probably for the consecration ceremony in 876, with a sacred relic known as the Sancta Camisia, supposed to have been a garment worn by Mary when she gave birth to Jesus Christ. It had been sent to Charlemagne as a gift from the Empress Irene of Byzantium. Admittedly, some texts declare that Mary wore it at the time of the Annunciation, so apparently even in medieval times there was some confusion. However, because of the firm belief that saints intercede through their earthly relics, then as the devotion to Mary grew in the Western Church, especially during the 12th and 13th centuries, so Chartres grew in importance as a pilgrimage shrine and was thought of as the earthly palace of the Queen of Heaven.

The citizens of Chartres knew not only that the relic was a considerable source of income for them, but also that they and their city were protected through it by Mary. Thus in 911, when Chartres was besieged by another Viking, named Rollon, Bishop Gantelme ordered the relic to be displayed upon the city ramparts. Rollon fled, made his peace with King Charles III, was converted to Christianity and invested as first Duke of Normandy.

It was probably during the 980s that Fulbert, a brilliant scholar, came to Chartres from the Reims Cathedral School, where his master had been Gerbert d'Aurillac, the future Pope Silvester II, and taught first at the Chartres Benedictine School of Saint-Père-en-Vallée outside the city walls and then, from about 990 until his death in 1028, at the Chartres Cathedral School, which he established as one of the foremost scholastic institutions of medieval Europe for the next two centuries, until the founding of the University of Paris caused this and other similar schools to decline. Through his friendship with Pope Silvester, Fulbert called upon the Western Church to establish a Marial liturgy,

9

and his writings undoubtedly influenced St Bernard in the following century. He taught medicine and introduced the astrolabe into medieval Europe, gaining an international reputation as the 'Venerable Socrates of the Chartres Academy'.

Amongst his most illustrious successors were Ivo of Chartres (1040–1117) and the neo-Platonist Bernard of Chartres, chancellor from about 1119 until 1124, who thought of the scholars of his time as dwarfs perched upon the shoulders of giants, the philosophers of antiquity, an idea later applied to the evangelists carried by the prophets beneath the South Rose window. Thierry of Chartres, Bernard's younger brother, compiled a Heptateuchon, or encyclopaedia of the seven liberal arts, and wrote: 'Philosophy has two principal instruments, the mind and its expression. The mind is enlightened by the Quadrivium (arithmetic, geometry, astronomy and music), its expression, elegant, reasonable, ornate, is provided by the Trivium (grammar, rhetoric and dialectic).' A few years later, these seven liberal arts, accompanied by those authors who best illustrated each, were sculpted on the Royal Portal of Chartres Cathedral.

A pupil of Bernard, Gilbert de la Porée, succeeded him as chancellor in 1124 until 1141, when he moved to Paris, and then became bishop of Poitiers. He is best known, perhaps, for his dispute with St Bernard of Clairvaux, arising from his application of Platonic metaphysical doctrines to the theology of the Trinity. Another pupil of Bernard of Chartres, William of Conches, like his master commented upon the relationships between Greek philosophy and the Scriptures, between the Creation narrative, for example, in the Book of Genesis and in Plato's *Timaeus*. A distinguished grammarian, he tutored, amongst other illustrious pupils, the future Henry II of England, whose quarrel with Thomas Becket was witnessed by yet another famous Chartres scholar, an Englishman, John of Salisbury (1110–80). Educated in Paris and Chartres, by Peter Abelard and William of Conches, he became both secretary and friend to Thomas and was exiled with him in France; and although he was canon for a time at Exeter Cathedral, he ended his life as bishop of Chartres and one of the most respected humanists of the 12th century.

Like John of Salisbury, Fulbert was an outstanding scholar who ended his life as bishop of Chartres. He was enthroned in 1006, and it was during his episcopate, on the night of 7 September 1020, that a fire destroyed most of the Carolingian cathedral. In order to build a much vaster and more magnificent edifice it was necessary to raise funds, so Fulbert wrote to King Robert requesting financial aid, and similar letters were addressed to William V,

Duke of Aquitaine, Richard, Duke of Normandy, and Eudes II, Count of Chartres-Blois. The English chronicler William of Malmesbury noted that of all the churches abroad endowed by Canute, King of England and Denmark, that of Chartres received the most generous gifts.

The small Carolingian martyrium, known as St Lubin's crypt, originally beneath a raised choir, was kept. Around it Fulbert's architect, Beranger, constructed a second and much vaster U-shaped Romanesque crypt, with very long galleries where pilgrims could spend the night and be tended if they were sick. This crypt, still the largest in France, is all that has survived from Fulbert's cathedral, although

BELOW: *A miniature, probably from the 11th century and attributed to André de Mici, showing Fulbert, with a crozier, inside his cathedral which had a nave, an aisle, apsidal chapels, a north-west tower (destroyed by fire in 1030) and a western open porch supporting a high bell-tower, which burnt down in 1134.*

RIGHT: *A 12th-century mural in Fulbert's crypt, showing (on the left) St Giles celebrating a Mass for the forgiveness of a sin that Charles (spelt KAROLUS) Martel dared not confess. However, in spite of the anachronism, for St Giles died in 725, it is usually Martel's grandson Charlemagne who is represented in this scene, because he was accused of having had an incestuous relationship with one of his sisters.*

BELOW: *St Fulbert with his cathedral. A detail, inspired by the André de Mici miniature, from the St Fulbert window, donated by the American Architects' Association and made by François Lorin, a Chartres glassmaker, in 1954.*

from archaeological research and from a miniature by André de Mici it is known that when it was consecrated, on 17 October 1037, it was the same width as the present Gothic structure, somewhat shorter and much lower, with nave, aisles, three apsidal chapels and a west porch supporting a bell-tower, such as still exists at Saint-Benoît-sur-Loire.

A century later, during the episcopates of Geoffrey de Lèves (1115–49) and Goslein de Musy (1149–56), Fulbert's cathedral was extended westwards. First, after another fire in 1134 had damaged the western parts of the church, Fulbert's porch and bell-tower were demolished and a new free-standing single north-west tower constructed, with a wooden steeple. (Successive wooden steeples burnt, until 1507 when Jehan de Beauce was commissioned to construct the present flamboyant structure.) During the next four decades, a south-west tower was built, with an elegantly proportioned octagonal steeple; the pilgrimage crypts were lengthened into the two new towers, and between them a magnificent portal – the Royal Portal – was constructed, surmounted by three high lancet windows, above which may still be seen a broken arch, indicating the approximate elevation of the Romanesque cathedral, which had no rose window.

1194–1260: THE GOTHIC CATHEDRAL

During the night of 10 June 1194, yet another fire destroyed most of the illustrious city of Chartres, and Fulbert's cathedral was very severely damaged. The tragedy is narrated in *Les Miracles de Nostre-Dame de Chartres*, a mid-13th-century translation by Jehan le Marchand of an earlier Latin text. At first, the chronicler writes, the people despaired because they believed that the precious relic had also burnt and therefore that Mary's protection of the city was lost, but on the third day after the fire Cardinal Melior, a papal legate, was exhorting the people to rebuild when a procession appeared with the relic safe, having apparently been taken by priests into the Carolingian crypt beneath the choir. The cardinal then declared that this was a sign from Mary that she desired a more magnificent church, and great enthusiasm was immediately aroused for the reconstruction.

People gathered voluntarily in the quarries at Berchères and, in thousands, praying and chanting, dragged carts laden with stone a distance of five miles to the building site. Bishop Regnault de Mouçon and the cathedral Chapter gave up the most part of their considerable income for the next five years for the building of the new cathedral. King Philip Augustus, who visited Chartres in 1210, provided each year the funds for the construction of the North Porch. This practice was continued by his son, Louis VIII, whose queen, Blanche of Castile, granddaughter of Eleanor of Aquitaine and Henry II Plantagenet, and regent of France from 1226 to 1236, donated the North Rose window and

lancets. Their son, Saint Louis, gave a rood-screen, unfortunately demolished by the clergy in the 18th century. Although he was at war with Philip Augustus, Richard Coeur de Lion permitted priests to raise funds in England. Other gifts came from a king of Castile, probably Ferdinand III, who is portrayed in one of the choir rose windows, as are Prince Louis of France, son of Philip Augustus, and other mounted knights in armour, all facing east in the direction of the crusades and bearing the coats of arms of their noble families, Beaumont, Courtenay and Montfort. Pierre Mauclerc, Count of Dreux and Duke of Brittany, gave the South Rose and lancets, and other windows in the choir and south ambulatory were given by the Count of Chartres, Thibault VI.

With the decline of the feudal system, there had been a drifting away from the land towards the developing towns, which then became increasingly important trading centres. Chartres was no exception, and new ramparts had been constructed just before the 1194 fire to contain the growing population. The merchant brotherhoods donated forty-three windows for the new cathedral, and their 'signatures', in more than a hundred scenes, have caught them timelessly in their occupations and provide a fascinating insight into everyday life in the early 13th century. Money-changers, with coins and scales, exchange over a bench – hence their nickname *banquiers* (bankers); fishmongers, beneath a colourful market parasol, dangle a cod before a customer; a vintner, hooded against the March winds, prunes his vine and bakers carry an

LEFT: *Jesus washing his disciples' feet, walking to Emmaus and at supper at Emmaus. Details from the capitals of the Royal Portal.*

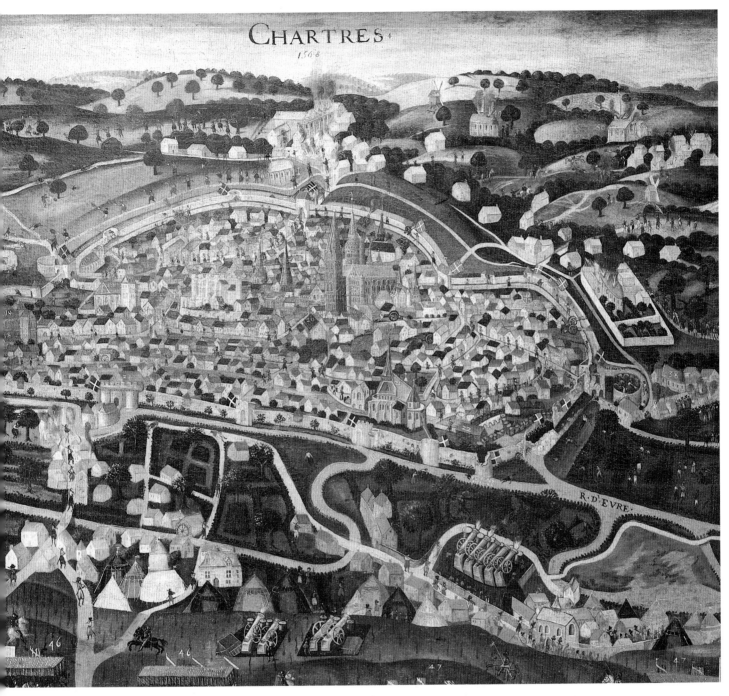

CHARTRES
1568

R. D'EVRE.

enormous basket of loaves high in the choir, signifi- cantly above the altar, where bread is used in the Holy Mass. So generous and continuous were these gifts pouring in, that the debris of the ruined cathe- dral was soon cleared and master builders and craftsmen (although no names have survived) were able to set up their workshops and begin the task of reconstruction. They built so quickly that by 1222 William the Breton could write in his court chronicle, the Philippis: 'None can be found in the whole world that would equal its structure, its size and decor ... the mother of Christ has a special love for this one church ... None is shining so brightly than this nowadays rising anew and com- plete, with dressed stone, already finished up to the level of the roof.'

Although most of the cathedral was completed by 1223, the north transept was still unfinished in 1230, and by 1260 the project of building nine steeples was abandoned. At last, on 24 October 1260, Chartres Cathedral was consecrated 'the Cathedral Church of the Assumption of Our Lady', but, in spite of the final delay, the speed with which the Gothic structure was rebuilt accounts for its architectural homogeneity and especially its icono- graphic unity.

ABOVE: *Chartres besieged by the Hugenot army in 1568. The cathedral dominates the medieval walled city. (Courtesy of the Chartres museum.)*

13

THE DONORS' WINDOWS

ABOVE: *The apothecaries and haberdashers were donors of the Miracles of St Nicholas window in the north aisle.*

RIGHT: *Farriers shoeing a horse, set in a wooden frame and held firmly by its bridle and a hind leg in order to prevent it kicking. Donors of the symbolic window of the Redemption.*

BELOW: *Wheelwrights constructing a wooden wheel. Noah window. North aisle.*

BELOW: *A market scene. A customer makes a purchase from a fishmonger. Detail from the St Anthony and St Paul the Anchorite window, south ambulatory.*

ABOVE: *Butchers at a trestle table with slabs of meat and a calf's head. A customer is pointing to the slice he wishes to buy, and the butcher's sign, a pig's carcass, is hanging from a nail. Donors of the Miracles of Mary window.*

TOP: *A customer being served by a shoemaker. Detail from the Assumption window.*

RIGHT: *Carpenters, donors of the Noah window in the north aisle, shaping wood.*

RIGHT: *A group of shoemakers offering a stained-glass window to the cathedral. Detail from the Good Samaritan window. South aisle.*

CHARTRES CATHEDRAL SINCE 1260

BELOW: *An aerial view of modern Chartres, still a medley of red and blue roofs as in the painting on page 13.*

After the addition of a vestry east of the north transept, the first major addition to the cathedral came in the form of the St Piat Chapel, built between 1324 and 1353, where pilgrims flocked to the saint's miraculous relic by climbing an elegant staircase opened up between the east and south-east apsidal chapels. Today, the St Piat Chapel exhibits the cathedral treasure, which includes fragments of the 13th-century rood-screen.

In 1413, Louis de Bourbon, Count of Vendôme, imprisoned by his brother Jacques and threatened with death and the confiscation of his estates, made a vow to Our Lady to raise a chapel in her honour in Chartres Cathedral upon his release. Construction

of the Vendôme Chapel, opened up in the south aisle of the nave, began in 1417, although Louis had meanwhile been captured again, this time by Henry V Plantagenet, at the Battle of Agincourt. Recognized as successor to the French throne by the Treaty of Troyes in 1420, Henry walked barefooted, candle in hand, from Dreux to Chartres on Assumption Day of that year.

It was largely due to the generosity of Louis XII, who gave 2,000 livres, and the publishing of indulgences by the papal legate, Cardinal Georges d'Amboise, to all those who helped, whether by their labours or offerings, that work was begun in 1507 upon the construction of a new stone steeple for the

RIGHT: *The St Piat Chapel, added in the early 14th century, now houses the cathedral treasure, which includes fragments of the 13th-century rood-screen given by Saint Louis and demolished in the 18th century by the clergy.*

RIGHT: *Mary sewing. An enchanting sculpture by Jean Soulas from the choir screen, about 1520.*

BELOW: *The south ambulatory of the cathedral, showing part of the choir screen constructed by Jehan de Beauce between 1514 and 1529. The 41 sculpted scenes took two centuries to complete and are the work of various artists. The screen begins and ends with scenes from the life of Mary; in between are scenes from the life of Christ.*

north tower, the old wooden steeple covered in lead having burnt down. Jean Texier, known as Jehan de Beauce, was appointed architect and, after completing the new spire by 1513 in the richly ornate, flamboyant style of his day, he was commissioned to build a choir screen in the same style, which he began in 1514 and worked upon until his death in 1529. The sculpted groups within this screen, however, were not completed until the 18th century, but were added gradually depending upon the availability of funds.

After having survived the 16th-century wars of religion almost unharmed and passed through a comparatively uneventful 17th century, Chartres Cathedral then, in the latter half of the 18th century, suffered the greatest degradations and indignities of its history, firstly at the hands of the clergy, then at those of the revolutionaries. In 1753, the cathedral Chapter decided to 'modernize' the choir! The borders of several of the 13th-century choir windows were removed and plain glass inserted. In 1763, the rood-screen given by Saint Louis was demolished and wrought-iron gates took its place. Charles-Antoine Bridan sculpted the Assumption high altar in 1773, and eight of the choir windows and four in the transept were destroyed to let in more light.

During the French Revolution and the ensuing Terror, the rich cathedral treasure was despoiled, a constitutional clergy established, the much-revered wooden statue of Our Lady of the Crypt burnt in front of the Royal Portal on 20 December 1793, and the cathedral rededicated as a 'temple of reason'. All statues, inside and out, were to be destroyed, and it was even suggested that the entire cathedral should be demolished. Certain citizens, however, disapproved, including the architect Morin, who pointed out the difficulties involved! By 1795, the danger had passed, and in 1800, on the feast day of the Assumption, Mass was once more celebrated in the Cathedral of Our Lady of Chartres.

In 1836, the vast wooden framework known as *la forêt*, over the nave, choir and transept, burnt in a great fire caused by the carelessness of a workman. Fortunately, the stone vaults withstood the calamity, and a new cast-iron framework, covered with copper, was completed by 1841.

During the 20th-century world wars the glass was dismantled and the cathedral survived unscathed. Since 1968 a vast restoration programme has been undertaken to enable future generations, like the pilgrims of the past, to hear Chartres speak of beauty and truth, time and eternity.

RIGHT: *The superb achievement of the medieval builders of the Gothic cathedral can be appreciated to the full in this photograph. The Labyrinth, inlaid in the* *paving of the cathedral nave, is the largest and best preserved from medieval France. Pilgrims walked it, or went round on their knees, as a spiritual exercise.*

ARCHITECTURE

OPPOSITE: *Flying buttresses on the south side of the choir make a complex and delicate pattern.*

The remarkable speed – less than 30 years – with which most of Chartres Cathedral was reconstructed after the 1194 catastrophe accounts for its architectural and iconographic unity. Its dimensions, however, except for the elevation and the addition of the very wide transept, were determined by those parts which survived the fire. The entire substructure was kept. Although revaulted in the 18th century, the small mid-9th-century martyrium beneath the choir, with its massive rectangular piers and five apsidal openings (probably walled up after the 1020 fire), is still the oldest part of Chartres Cathedral. Around it, Fulbert's 11th-century crypt was consolidated, especially in the

BELOW: *A cut-away drawing of the cathedral showing the principal features of its architectural design.*

apse, by doubling the wall around the three wide barrel-vaulted chapels and adding smaller, heavily rib-vaulted ones between them. These alternating Romanesque and Gothic, wide and narrow, chapels in the crypt determined not only the semicircular apsidal form of the Gothic cathedral above, but also the disposition of its radiating chapels and the irregular spacing of the ambulatory piers, just as the long, groin-vaulted pilgrimage galleries built in the 1020s beneath the aisles of the Gothic structure determined its width and orientation.

It was similarly decided to keep the 12th-century western extension to Fulbert's cathedral, which had also survived the 1194 fire, the Royal Portal, its three lancet windows and the flanking towers. Both of these towers were built during the mid-12th-century 'transition' period; they are still Romanesque in their solidity, with large inner wall surfaces and, at their base, typical Romanesque chevroned rounded arches, especially at the entrance from the nave into their lower rooms, both of which, nevertheless, have early Gothic ribbed vaulting. The north-west tower, constructed during the 1130s, still has traditional Romanesque capitals with mythological confronted beasts and hunting

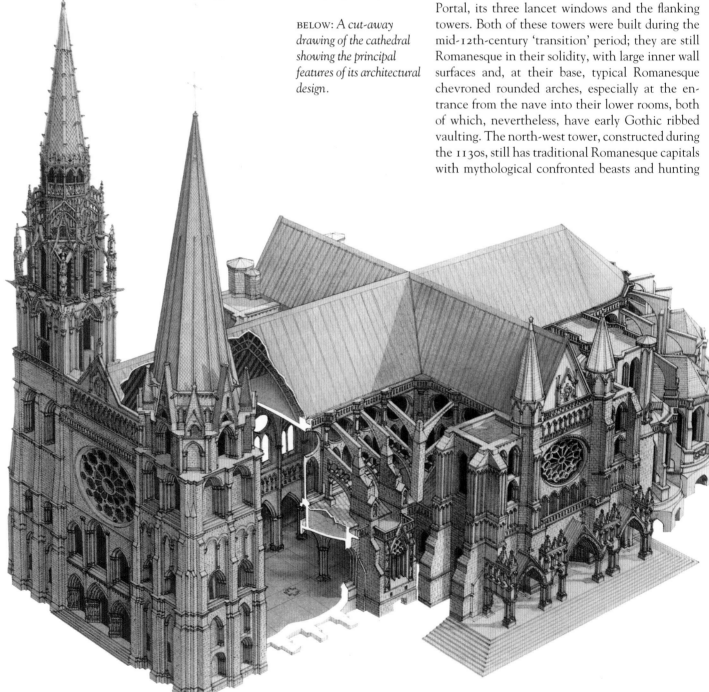

RIGHT: *Flying buttresses on the outside of the nave stabilize the thrust of the vaults on the inner wall.*

FAR RIGHT: *Buttresses outside the south nave with niches containing ecclesiastical figures.*

scenes of the type that St Bernard criticized as 'bizarre extravagance', whereas the south-west tower's capitals are more austerely decorated with acanthus leaves.

From the outside, both square towers appear similar in their lower stages, but the north-western one narrows sharply at the rose-window level with tapering buttresses which supported the wooden steeple that burnt in 1194. The south-west tower narrows more progressively, and its heavy wall structure is disguised by fluted columns that accentuate the upward movement towards the crown of pinnacles and gables, which in their turn conceal the subtle transition from the square to the octagon. It is here that the immense stone south steeple, the highest of its kind, begins its upward soar, combining strength with beauty, proportion and purity.

Just as the survival of the crypts determined the width of the Gothic cathedral, so the decision to keep the Royal Portal and the western towers determined its length. The Gothic builders did, however, expand in two ways; firstly by adding a very wide transept, so that the ground plan was altered from a U-shape to the cruciform plan, symbolic of the cross upon which Christ died, and secondly by building much higher, which was made possible by certain technical innovations.

The interior elevation is tripartite, with arcade, triforium and clerestory. The lower storey, or arcade, is made up of a series of pointed arches in the nave, transept and choir. They support the triforium, a narrow horizontal gallery with a row of

elegant columns giving a vertical rhythm, which replaces the heavy tribunes of earlier cathedrals such as those of Durham or Notre-Dame in Paris, which extended back over the whole width of the aisle. Above the triforium, the clerestory is lit by a series of double lancet windows with a cusped oculus above.

Alternating circular piers with octagonal shafts, and octagonal piers with circular shafts, built in drums, divide the nave, transept and choir into rectangular bays. The front shafts cut through the capitals decorated with crockets and foliage, thereby emphasizing verticality, and support transverse arches that span the structure from wall to wall. Crossed ribs, with central sculpted circular keystones, which still show traces of paint and gilt, then divide each rectangular canopy into quadripartite vaults. The transverse arches and ribs carry the considerable weight of the stone vaulting to the shoulder of the building inside and, where they meet the wall, flying buttresses outside (single along the nave and transept, double around the choir) stabilize their thrust.

This innovation, the combination of rectangular quadripartite vaults (replacing square sexpartite ones, such as at Notre-Dame in Paris) with flying buttresses, made it possible both to build higher and to open up the walls to a degree never before dared and to fill them with stained glass, so that they appear, like the walls of the Heavenly Jerusalem, to be 'garnished with all manner of precious stones' (Rev. 21:19,20).

OPPOSITE: *The quadripartite nave vaulting.*

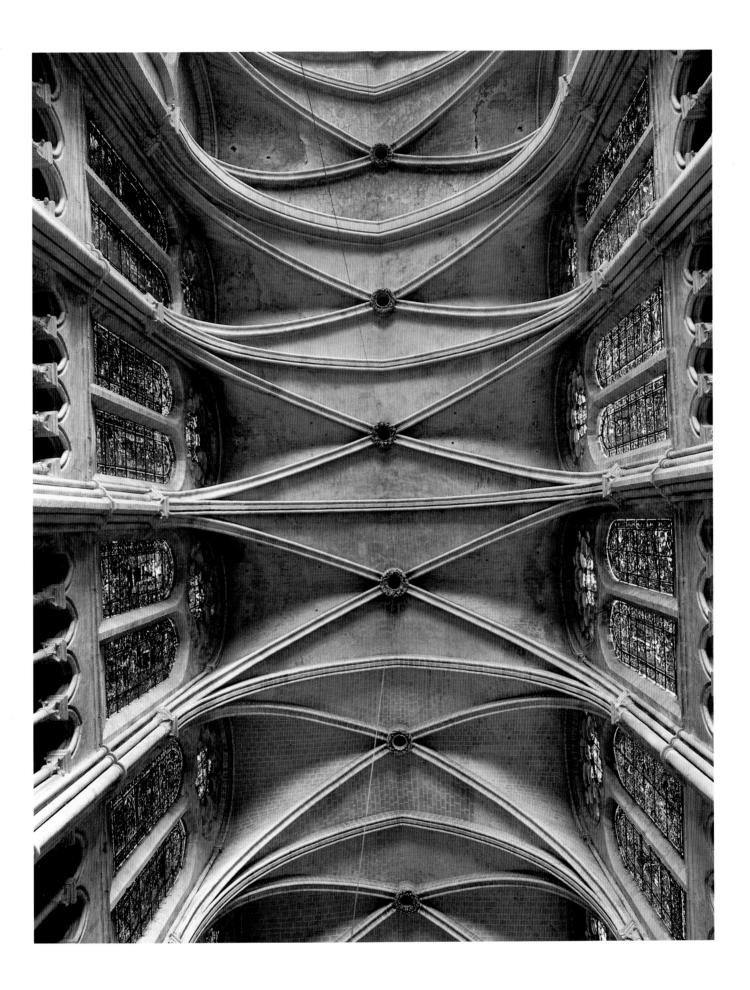

THE 12th CENTURY

THE ROYAL PORTAL

Constructed in the mid-12th century like its flanking towers, the Royal Portal shows similar signs of the transition from Romanesque to Gothic. Still in the Romanesque tradition are the elongated, rigid column figures. In contrast to the classic Gothic sculptures of the transept porches, which, like actors upon a stage, are detached from the architecture, these earlier figures are incorporated within the architecture of the portal, reminiscent of the performers in a medieval mystery play upon the cathedral steps. They stand stiffly, about to speak their parts: with raised hand, to proclaim a great prophecy, or, as queen of Judah, just to smile serenely in the knowledge that her lineage will bring forth the Christ.

Originally arranged 3-4-5-5-4-3, only nineteen have survived, and some are recent copies. At least three schools of sculptors worked upon these figures; the last two on the far left are attributed to the school of Etampes, and the group to the far right to the school of Saint-Denis. In both cases the sculpture is stylized, with deeply cut drapery folds and a certain bulky rigidity and mask-like quality. The figures of the central door, however, attributed to the 'Master of Chartres', although still rigidly columnar are more streamlined.

The statues lengthen from the door outwards although the heads remain at the same level; the drapery folds emphasize verticality, especially in the case of the queens with their braided hair and long sleeves, so that our eye is led upwards to the heads with their expressions of great serenity and dignity,

the outer substance reflecting the inner being. The crowned figures are extremely difficult to identify individually, but they probably represent Christ's royal ancestors, the kings and queens of Judah, and the uncrowned ones are probably His spiritual forebears – priests, prophets and patriarchs of the Old Testament.

The swirling drapery folds and tensions of pure Romanesque, such as at Vezelay or Autun, have gone. The Royal Portal of Chartres is almost static

ABOVE: *Aristotle. Royal Portal, right bay, outer left archivolt.*

RIGHT: *The Annunciation to the Shepherds. A detail from the lower lintel of the right bay of the Royal Portal.*

RIGHT: *The Last Supper, sculpted on the right buttress of the Royal Portal. Beneath the kneeling Judas is the mysterious inscription ROGERUS.*

PREVIOUS PAGE: *The Royal Portal, 1145–55.*

and highly ordered, being divided into practically equal halves by the horizontal frieze, so that the lower half, with its vertical column figures, appears to carry the upper half with its strong horizontal lintel lines.

The frieze is composed of almost two hundred figurines. The left part, from the central door to the north tower, begins with twelve apocryphal scenes from the life of Mary, leading to the Annunciation, Visitation and Nativity sculpted on the buttress capital, followed by the Annunciation to the Shepherds, the Adoration of the Magi and, on the extreme left, the Flight into Egypt and the Massacre of the Innocents, much of which is repeated above in the glass of the central lancet window.

The right part of the frieze mostly concerns the death and resurrection of Jesus, as does the window above. On the buttress capital this time is sculpted the Last Supper, followed (to the right) by the Kiss of Judas, whose stealthy movement breathes treachery. On the extreme right Christ washes His disciples' feet, then, resurrected, He walks to and sups at Emmaus and finally appears to the doubting Thomas who is reaching to touch his wounded side.

LEFT: *A queen of Judah and two other Old Testament figures. Column statues from the left jamb of the central bay of the Royal Portal, mid-12th century.*

ABOVE: *Detail from the Royal Portal frieze showing Christ betrayed by Judas.*

A further unity is given to the portal by the three Christ figures, each in a frontal position, in the three tympana: over the right door as a child on Mary's knee; over the left door ascending and over the central door triumphant at the end of time. The lateral bays each have two lintels, and the central bay only one. Beneath Mary and Child, the Incarnation cycle is sculpted once more; the Annunciation, then a very tender Visitation followed by the Nativity, in which the Child is exposed as upon an altar to symbolize His sacrificial pre-destination, and the Annunciation to the Shepherds. On the second lintel is one scene, the Presentation of the Christ Child at the Temple, in which the Child is once again placed upon an altar.

Beneath the ascending Christ, angels swoop downwards announcing His return. Surrounding Him in the archivolts are the zodiac signs with their corresponding monthly activities; around Mary and Child, wisdom incarnate, are sculpted the seven liberal arts with those scholars who best illustrated each art: from the apex downwards, to the left, are Geometry and Euclid, Rhetoric and Cicero, Dialectic and Aristotle; to the right are Arithmetic and Boethius, Astronomy and Ptolemy, Grammar and either Donatus or Priscian, beside whom are Pythagoras and Music, playing a tintinnabulum. Christ rules over all human endeavour, whether intellectual or manual: 'He changeth the times and the seasons: He removeth kings, and setteth up kings: He giveth wisdom unto the wise, and knowledge to them that know understanding' (Dan. 2:21).

The iconographic programme of the Royal Portal culminates over the central door with the Second Coming of Christ to judge the quick and the dead, assisted according to His promise (Matt. 19:28) by the twelve apostles beneath His feet in four seated groups of three, with the outer standing figures, Enoch and Elijah, who will return just before the end of time to convert all mankind. Then, beyond time, He will reign eternally, enthroned in the Heavenly Jerusalem, according to the Book of the Revelation. Around Him in the tympanum are the four apocalyptic animals symbolizing the four evangelists, and around them, in the archivolts, first angels, and then the twenty-four elders of the Apocalypse playing a variety of medieval musical instruments, and the beasts and the elders 'give glory and honour and thanks to Him that sat on the throne, who liveth for ever and ever'.

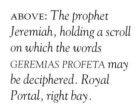

ABOVE: *The prophet Jeremiah, holding a scroll on which the words* GEREMIAS PROFETA *may be deciphered. Royal Portal, right bay.*

RIGHT: *April, the month of nature's rebirth, holding the branches of a tree covered with leaves and blossom. Royal Portal, left bay.*

LEFT: *Pythagoras and Donatus or Priscian. Royal Portal, right bay.*

RIGHT: *Old Testament figures from the right bay of the Royal Portal, left jamb.*

THE JESSE WINDOW

NUMERICAL REFERENCES
IN TEXT: *Bold numbers,
e.g. (8), refer to the plan
on page 4; ordinary
numbers, e.g. (12), to
the panels of the relevant
window diagram.*

BELOW: *A King of Judah.
Detail from the Jesse
window.*

Above the Royal Portal sculpture, and pro-grammed with it, are three lancet windows, among the oldest and most brilliant to have sur-vived from medieval Europe. Although cleaned, restored and releaded in the mid-1970s, they date from about 1150. Both in design and in meaning they form a triptych, proclaiming that the prophe-cies have been fulfilled, that the Christ came from the House of David in the conditions foretold, was sacrificed, but rose from the dead.

Although the Tree of Jesse theme probably began in 11th-century German miniatures, it took on a much more grandiose form, first in 1144 in a stained-glass window at the royal abbey of Saint-Denis under its famous abbot, Suger, then at Chartres and York in about 1150, before proliferat-ing elsewhere to become one of the most popular subjects in medieval monumental iconography. Almost nothing has survived of the York window, and the present one at Saint-Denis dates partly from the 19th century. This superbly luminous Chartres window is therefore the best-preserved early example of the theme, which was inspired by the great Messianic prophecy of Isaiah (11:1): 'And

there shall come forth a rod out of the stem of Jesse, and a branch shall grow out of his roots.'

Jesse, father of David, reclines at the base of the window upon a bed of white linen. He is wrapped in a bright red, yellow-bordered blanket and sleeps, his head upon a pillow and his right hand under his chin. His feet are bare, like those of prophets and evangelists, and he wears the Jewish conical cap. Above him a lamp hangs on a golden chain and a curtain flutters from a red semicircular arch, beyond which, in the spandrels, spreads the royal city of David, Bethlehem.

From Jesse's groin, the source of life, springs not a rod, but the trunk of a tree, in the centre of which the sap can be clearly seen rising through a succession of four kings of Judah, richly clad in red and green, yellow and purple, against a background of intense blue. They are seated frontally, grasping with both hands branches that spring from their feet and which subdivide to either side symmetrically in a curvilinear design to terminate in stylized foliage and flowers, some of which resemble the fleur-de-lis, adopted about that time as the royal emblem of the Capet kings. Although they carry neither attribute nor inscription, the four crowned figures probably represent David, Solomon, Roboam and Abia, the first in Matthew's long list of twice fourteen kings of Judah, Christ's royal ancestors.

Mary, and not Joseph, is the sixth figure in the tree, for she is the instrument of the Incarnation, bringing the seventh, who is Christ, her Son, the flower and the fruit of the tree. According to Tertullian in the 3rd century, St Jerome two centuries later, and St Fulbert of Chartres, if the prophetic stem (*radix*) is Jesse, then the rod (*virga*) represents Mary (*virgo*), and the flower (*flos*) is Christ.

Christ is seated at the summit of the tree, with cruciform nimbus and bare feet, surrounded by doves that symbolize the seven gifts of the Holy Spirit, for Isaiah had written: 'The spirit of the Lord shall rest upon him, the spirit of wisdom and understanding, the spirit of counsel and fortitude, the spirit of knowledge and godliness, and he shall be filled with the spirit of the fear of the Lord' (Isa. 11:2).

Contained within red half-circles on either side of the figures in the tree, and turned towards them, are twice seven Old Testament prophets bearing scrolls on which their names are written. From the top and from left to right, they are Habakkuk and Zephaniah, Isaiah and Daniel, Moses and Balaam, Zechariah and Joel, Ezekiel and Micah, Samuel and Amos, Nahum and Hosea.

Thus, Christ's spiritual forebears frame His ancestors of the flesh and prepare for the narrative of the Incarnation, the temporal fulfilment of the prophecies, in the adjacent central lancet window.

LEFT: *The Jesse window, about 1150. From the groin of Jesse, who reclines at the foot of the window, springs a stem in the branches of which sit four kings of Judah, then Mary, and Jesus at the top, surrounded by seven doves symbolizing the seven gifts of the Holy Spirit. In the border are twice seven Old Testament prophets, who foretold that the Christ would come from the House of David.*

THE INCARNATION WINDOW

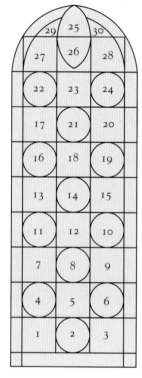

Mounted against a square armature, the twenty-four narrative scenes of this window are set within alternating red squares and blue circles. The numbering of the scenes corresponds to that on the plan of the window (*left*).

1 The Annunciation

In this first panel, the angel Gabriel with two fingers raised in salutation, and carrying a herald's sceptre like Mercury, announces to Mary, 'Behold, thou shalt conceive in thy womb, and bring forth a son, and shalt call his name Jesus.' Mary has risen from her seat, and her gesture expresses surprise.

2 The Visitation

Gabriel also announced that Mary's cousin, Elizabeth, had conceived a son in old age. So Mary came 'to the house of Zacharias, and saluted Elizabeth. And it came to pass that when Elizabeth heard the salutation of Mary, the babe leaped in her womb.'

Elizabeth, six months with child, stands in red and green with parted hands to greet her young cousin. Elizabeth's condition and the leap of John the Baptist in her womb were signs to Mary that she, although virgin, was likewise with child.

3 The Nativity

At birth, the Christ Child is placed not in a homely manger but, as on the Royal Portal, sacramentally upon an altar, here represented flat-topped and supported by sculpted columns, to symbolize that His blood and flesh, the *corpus verum*, are present in the Eucharist. It was written in the *Glossa ordinaria*, a 10th-century compilation of the Biblical commentaries of the Church Fathers, used widely in the monastic and cathedral schools: 'the cradle in which He sleeps is the very altar of sacrifice'. Mary, in a half-sitting position, rests upon a couch beneath a blue cover, pointing to her child wrapped in swaddling clothes. Behind Him are the traditional

RIGHT: *The Nativity (3), from the Incarnation window. The Christ Child is shown upon an altar, symbolizing that His blood and flesh are present in the Eucharist.*

OPPOSITE: *The Incarnation window.*

ox and ass, inspired from the apocryphal Gospel of the Pseudo-Matthew: 'The Virgin placed her child in a crib, and the ox and the ass adored Him. Thus was the prophecy of Isaiah fulfilled which foretold: "The ox knoweth his master and the ass his master's crib".' Joseph, at the foot of Mary's bed, appears to be asleep, like Jesse, with his right hand supporting his chin. A lamp, again reminiscent of the adjacent Jesse panel, hangs between parted curtains. In the upper right corner shines the star of Bethlehem that will guide the Magi.

4 Annunciation to the Shepherds
'And there were in the same country shepherds abiding in the fields.' All three wear short peasant smocks and have crooks. Between them, the dogs and masters look upwards in amazement at the swooping angels, who reveal to them that in the city of David 'a saviour is born, which is Christ the Lord'.

5–10 Adoration of the Magi: the Epiphany
Meanwhile, three wise men or, more precisely, astronomer-priests come from the east to Jerusalem, with pilgrim staffs. Two are bearded, the other youthful with a slight moustache, and all are crowned, although Matthew's narrative makes no mention of kings. However, Isaiah had prophesied: 'And the Gentiles shall come to thy light, and kings to the brightness of thy rising' (Isa. 60:3). First (5 and 6), they stand before Herod, who is seated, holding a sceptre, beneath two arches representing his palace, and they ask, 'Where is he that is born King of the Jews? For we have seen his star in the east, and are come to worship him ... and Herod was troubled ... and he gathered all the chief priests and scribes of the people together, and he demanded of them, where Christ should be born.' Two figures beneath the left arch agitatedly consult the Scriptures, and answer him, saying, 'In Bethlehem of Judaea; for thus it is written by the prophet' (Matt. 2:5 and Micah 5:2).

The Magi depart (7), following their star, each displaying a coin with curious imitation Hebraic inscriptions, and come to adore the Christ Child, seated upon His mother's lap, blessing. As on the Royal Portal, Mary is enthroned beneath a balda-quin (8), as the mother of the *Logos* (Word) made flesh. To the right (9), the Magi leave, still follow-ing the star, one showing his empty hand. Their visit signifies the Gentiles' recognition that God has manifested himself incarnate (the Epiphany) to all mankind in the form of Jesus, the Christ, and was inspired not only by Isaiah 60:3 but also by Psalm 72:10, where it is foretold that 'the kings of Tashish and of the isles shall bring presents; the kings of Sheba and Seba shall offer gifts. Yea, all kings shall

LEFT: *The Massacre of the Innocents (14 and 15), from the Incarnation window.*

fall down before him; all nations shall serve him.' The four kings in the psalm were reduced to three to correspond with the three gifts spoken of by St Matthew, gold to symbolize Christ's royalty, myrrh His mortality, and frankincense His divinity.

'And being warned of God in a dream (10) that they should not return to Herod, they departed into their own country another way.' An angel awakens one of the bearded Magi by touching his shoulder, whilst the others sleep.

11–12 The Presentation at the Temple

In accordance with Jewish law (Exodus 13:2), because Jesus was a first-born son and therefore belonged to Yahveh, he had to be presented at the temple and the sacrifice made of 'a pair of turtle-doves, or two young pigeons'. Likewise, on the for-tieth day after childbirth, Mary had to undergo the Jewish rite of Purification (Leviticus 12:1) which in the Christian liturgy is celebrated on 2 February, Candlemas. The first of the three women accom-panying Mary (11) carries turtle-doves, but the other two hold candles, for since the 5th century at least the feast of Candlemas has been celebrated with a procession of lights, perhaps inspired by Luke 2:32, 'a light to lighten the Gentiles', words spoken by Simeon, portrayed (12) elderly and bearded and with bare feet as a prophet, for he foretold Christ's future sufferings. Thus the temple altar upon which the Child is presented symbolizes the Christian altar upon which the Redeemer's sacrifice will be accomplished.

13–15 The Massacre of the Holy Innocents

'Then Herod, when he saw that he was mocked of the wise men, was exceeding wroth, and sent forth, and slew all the children that were in Bethle-hem from two years old and under.' Beneath an arch, as lower in the window (5), Herod is

enthroned, holding a sceptre. Cross-legged, mous-tached, bull-necked, he orders his soldiers, swords unsheathed, to murder the Innocents. One mother, in blue, kneels mourning her dead infant; another, standing in white, solemnly offers her child to a ferocious, snarling soldier who withdraws his sword blood-stained from the child's abdomen, and the child, with open arms, accepts martyrdom, the second baptism, which, according to St Ignatius of Antioch, is in blood as the first is in water.

16 The Flight into Egypt

'The angel of the Lord appeareth to Joseph in a dream, saying, arise and take the young child, and his mother and flee into Egypt . . . that it might be fulfilled which was spoken of by the prophet [Hosea 11:1] saying, out of Egypt have I called my son.'

In traditional style, Joseph leads a white mule by its bridle, from left to right. He carries a small bundle tied upon a staff across his shoulder, and looks back towards Mary, who journeys side-saddle with the Child enthroned upon her lap, in a similar frontal position to His mother. She holds a palm branch, which she appears to have taken from the tree they are passing. The Pseudo-Matthew relates how the Christ Child ordered a palm tree to bend down and give of its fruit, and how water gushed from its roots. In gratitude He promised the palm tree that one of its shoots would be planted in the Heavenly Jerusalem, and this is evidently a link with His entry into the earthly Jerusalem on Palm Sunday.

17 The Falling Idols

The Evangelium of the Pseudo-Matthew also narrates, as does the Arabian Gospel of the Child-hood of Christ, the arrival of the Holy Family at Sotinen, where Jesus caused the idols to fall in the heathen temples, for Isaiah had foretold: 'Behold,

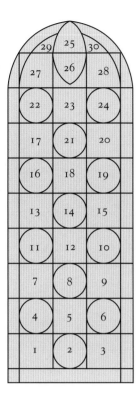

the Lord rideth upon a swift cloud, and shall come into Egypt; and the idols of Egypt shall be moved at his presence' (Isa. 19:1). Two idols, one of gold, the other of silver, topple from their pedestals with bent knees and outstretched arms, as though human. Above them, lamps hang from two arches supported by four columns with sculpted capitals, within crenellated walls and towers in the foreground, and other edifices above.

18–19 The Holy Family Welcomed at Sotinen (or Return to Nazareth?)

It is probably again the city of Sotinen which is so remarkably represented in the sixth central panel (18), with ramparts, streets, turrets and towers, houses with windows and hinged, nail-studded doors, and a high red city gate before which Aphrodisius, the governor, and a great retinue stand 'to welcome and worship him who possesses such powers over the gods'. Joseph, as before, leads (19), but no longer looks back, and the Christ Child,

again seated frontally upon His mother's lap, raises His hand in blessing. If this were the return from Egypt, and the city Nazareth, then the Child would be shown older and, like Mary, on foot, for it was believed that the Holy Family stayed seven years in Egypt before returning to Nazareth. After the Adoration of the Magi, the acclamation of Jesus at Sotinen in Egypt was commonly interpreted as the second revelation of His divinity to the Gentiles.

20 Joseph's Dream

Joseph appears to sleep profoundly, indoors, as indicated by the arch above him from which hangs the customary curtain and lighted lamp. An angel with a herald's sceptre gently touches his shoulder as though to awaken him.

Unfortunately, however, because the original disposition of the twenty-four panels is not known, the present order having been decided upon for aesthetic reasons during the 1897–9 restoration, it cannot be ascertained whether this scene refers to

RIGHT: *Joseph leads a white mule which carries Mary with the Child on her lap (16).*

ABOVE: *The city of Sotinen in Egypt (18), to which the Holy Family is welcomed by the governor and his retinue.*

thy king cometh unto thee meek, and sitting upon an ass.' Unusually, but as in a similar window at Bourges, it is Jesus who carries a palm branch, as Mary did during the flight into Egypt, whilst the apostles grouped behind Him mostly carry books. Beneath Jesus the ground is strewn with more palm branches and with garments, for the branch of palm was, in antiquity, a symbol not only of peace, but also of victory, and the spreading of garments upon the ground was a customary way of hailing the anointed king (2 Kgs. 9:13). Christ's hand is raised in blessing as the citizens of Jerusalem emerge from the city gate, waving palm branches. Heads appear over the crenellated and turreted walls of the city, and the children leap and dance excitedly upon the roof-tops. 'And the multitudes that went before, and that followed, cried, saying, Hosanna to the Son of David: Blessed is he that cometh in the name of the Lord' (Matt.21:9). Thus do the people of Jerusalem greet Jesus in the very words of Psalm 118:26, and hail Him as the Lord's anointed. Just as when He arrived at Sotinen the people did Him homage because they had witnessed His power over their heathen gods, so the citizens of Jerusalem acknowledge Him as the Christ, because of the power He revealed over death by raising Lazarus.

Joseph's second dream, in which he was commanded to flee into Egypt, or the third, after Herod's death, when he was told that it was safe to return.

21 The Baptism of Jesus Christ

Jesus stands naked in the waters of the river Jordan. On his right, John the Baptist, bare-footed and with raised hand, appears to be pronouncing the words: 'Behold the Lamb of God, which taketh away the sin of the world.' On Jesus's left is an angel holding a tunic. 'And it came to pass that Jesus being baptized ... the heaven was opened, and the Holy Ghost descended in a bodily shape like a dove upon him, and a voice came from heaven which said, Thou art my beloved Son; in thee I am well pleased.'

Thus the descent of the Holy Ghost in the form of a dove at the baptism of Jesus, and the voice proclaiming Him the Son of God, has the same significance as the star which appeared to the Magi to lead them to the Christ Child. Both the dove and star were visible signs to humanity that God was incarnate in the form of the Son.

22–24 Christ's Entry into Jerusalem

Seated upon a white donkey, like Mary during the flight into Egypt in the two lower scenes, Jesus arrives in triumph at Jerusalem, 'that it might be fulfilled which was spoken by the prophet [Zech. 9:9], saying, Tell ye the daughter of Sion, Behold,

25–30 Mary Enthroned (Sedes Sapientiae)

Mary is given the place of honour at the summit of the window. She is seated within a large mandorla upon her celestial throne holding two flowering sceptres, for she is doubly queen: Queen of Heaven, where she is enthroned, says the *Speculum Beatae Mariae*, in the midst of the angels, and of Earth, where she constantly manifests her power. She is the queen who carries the king of the world; she is the throne of Solomon, wrote the early Christian doctors, for her Child, the *Logos*, wisdom incarnate, sits upon her as upon a throne. In His left hand, the Child holds a book, whilst the right hand is raised, showing Him to be divine wisdom.

On either side, two angels, clothed in blue and white and holding sceptres, appear to do homage before the celestial throne, and in the spandrels above them, to the right of Mary and the Child, the sun, with the face of a young man, shines through clouds; to their left, the moon is shown as a crescent held by a woman wearing a blue veil. Both sun and moon were associated with Mary, because it is written in the Book of the Revelation (12:1): 'And there appeared a great wonder in Heaven: a woman clothed with the sun, and the moon under her feet.' According to St Augustine, the sun and moon also refer to the Old and New Testaments, for as the moon receives light from the sun, so the Law of Moses is unveiled and enlightened by the Gospels.

The Passion and Resurrection Window

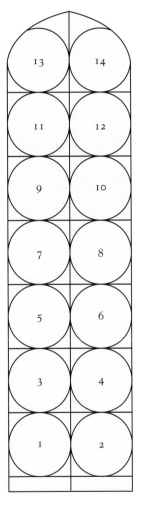

The fourteen panels of this window are all set within double circles of pearl-like white dots, so that the composition of many of the scenes depicted is curvilinear in design. The two lowest panels represent Christ's Transfiguration on Mount Tabor, thereby introducing the narrative of His Passion and Resurrection by showing that He had foreknowledge of both.

1–2 The Transfiguration

Jesus stands (1) at the centre of multiple, variously coloured mandorlas, and is lit, as in earlier Byzantine representations, by eight spokes of light. Peter, in white, John, the central beardless figure, and James 'fell on their faces and were sore afraid' (Matt. 17:6), and saw Him speaking with Moses, carrying the tables of the law, and Elijah, who 'appeared in glory, and spake of His decease which He should accomplish at Jerusalem' (Luke 9:31). Peter, half-sitting, is saying: 'Let us build three tabernacles; one for thee, one for Moses and one for Elijah.' Two of the greatest figures in Jewish history, Moses and Elijah, represent the Law and Prophecy, which were fulfilled in Jesus Christ.

A bright cloud overshadowed them (2) and, as at Christ's baptism, a voice out of the cloud proclaimed, 'This is my Son in whom I am well pleased', and Jesus, with raised hand, said 'Tell this vision to no man until the Son of Man is risen from the dead.' Thus, both the Incarnation and Passion windows begin with a revelation of Christ's divinity. Pope Leo the Great declared that 'the Incarnation of the *Logos* effected by the Holy Ghost through Mary and the Transfiguration which took place on Tabor proclaim that Christ is the Son of God and that He was sent from heaven. They vouch for the world-redeeming power of His victory won in the sign of the cross.'

3 The Last Supper

With His apostles, Jesus celebrated the Jewish feast of the Passover, commemorating the deliverance of the Jews from Egypt, and established the Eucharist as a deliverance from sin. Dressed in mauve, He is the central figure behind a table upon which are set several objects, including a red jug of wine, a dish with a red fish and, on the extreme right, a round white loaf. Since early Christian times, the miraculous multiplication of the loaves and the fishes and the feeding of the multitude was considered the most important New Testament prototype of the Last Supper and the establishment of the Eucharist, so that fish, as well as bread and wine, forms a part of the last meal. The fish was also considered as a symbol for Jesus himself. The Greek word *Ichthys* (fish) is an acrostic, *Iesous Chrystos Theou Hyious*

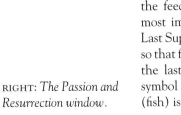

RIGHT: *The Passion and Resurrection window*.

ABOVE (left): *The Last Supper (3). Jesus gives a blessing as He offers bread to Judas, who is stealing a fish from the table. Detail from the Passion and Resurrection window.*

ABOVE (right): *Jesus washing His disciples' feet (4). Detail from the Passion and Resurrection window.*

Soter (Jesus Christ, Son of God, Redeemer). With Jesus are seven apostles, three to either side of Him, and Judas, separate, in front of the table. Whilst accepting, open-mouthed, the broken bread that Jesus offers him, he is taking the fish from the table. This refers to a popular scene in one of the Passion plays, in which Judas, having stolen a fish, is branded a thief.

4 The Washing of the Disciples' Feet

After the meal, Jesus 'arose, and took a white apron, and girded Himself. After that He poureth water into a basin, and began to wash His disciples' feet', which was an ancient custom, usually performed by slaves, but by Jesus as an act of humility. With His apostles grouped to either side of Him, He kneels before Peter, who is seated, and washes his leg over a yellow basin. Peter, touching his forehead, appears to be saying, 'Lord not my feet only, but also my hands and my head', just as David had said before him, 'Wash me thoroughly from my iniquity' (Ps. 51:2). Naturally, from early Christian times, the washing of the disciples' feet was understood to be a purification, like baptism. In the 4th century St Ambrose argued that baptism purged everyday sins and the washing of the feet abolished original sin, whereas St Bernard, in his *De cena Domini*, speaks of washing the feet as a sacrament for the forgiveness of everyday sins.

5 The Betrayal

A succession of events – the kiss of Judas, the seizure of Christ and the cutting off of Malchus's ear – are here combined in a bustling, violent composition. In the midst of this turbulent action Jesus stands calm and unresisting. Judas, again in green and yellow, approaches Him from the left, with up-turned chin and parted lips about to kiss. Behind him one of the guards, with a green helmet, holds a flaming torch. Malchus, to the right, dressed in a short yellow servant's tunic, grasps Jesus by the arm, and Peter, with a red halo, on the extreme right, is about to cut off his ear.

6 The Flagellation

Jesus's physical sufferings began with the prelude to crucifixion according to Roman law: flagellation. He is tied by His feet and hands to a yellow column, naked to the waist and wearing the crown of thorns, green against a red halo, beside which is the inscription INRI. Two scourgers flog Him viciously, brandishing great whips, their knees bent, their arm actions aggressive; and the face of the left figure is contorted and purple with rage.

7 The Crucifixion

Grief-stricken, Mary to her Son's right and John the Apostle to His left contemplate Jesus upon the cross. Although the blood trickles from His five wounds, the closed eyes, the sideways tilt of His head and the limp body sagging at the hips all signify death. The wood of the cross, however, by virtue of the vivifying qualities of Christ's blood, has become a living green bordered with red. A very popular anthem, known in the 12th century, begins, 'O crux, viride lignum', for it was commonly

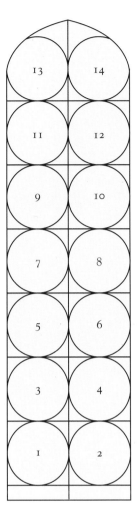

believed that the 'true' cross was made from the Tree of Life, which had grown in Paradise. Thus, of the two trees of the Garden of Eden, one brought about death, and the other, life.

8 The Deposition

Joseph of Arimathea supports Christ's limp body as Nicodemus, dressed in yellow and kneeling, draws the nails from His feet with tongs. Mary takes her Son's hands in hers, whilst John again stands in an attitude of grief. Joseph, as a member of the San-hedrin, and Nicodemus the Pharisee both wear Jewish head-dress.

9 The Anointing

Before entombment, in compliance with Jewish custom, the body of Jesus was wound in linen clothes and anointed with spices. Watched by Mary (upper left with a red halo), and John (upper right), Joseph of Arimathea, bare-headed, on the far left, and perhaps Nicodemus, on the far right, lower Jesus in a white shroud, either onto the anointing stone or into a sarcophagus, supported by four columns. One of the two central figures is wrapping Christ's body in purple linen, while the other, a yellow cup in his left hand, is rubbing Christ's chest with oils, a mixture of myrrh and aloes brought by Nicodemus.

10–14 The Resurrection

Before the 13th century, Christ's Resurrection itself was not usually represented, but only implied, by the visit of holy women to His sepulchre, where they found the tomb empty. Mary Magdalene, Mary the mother of James, and Salome (10), carrying vases of perfume, have entered the sepulchre, lit by three suspended lamps. The angel of the Lord, seated, with green wings, red face, hands and feet, 'his raiment white as snow', points to the empty tomb and the shroud hanging from it. At the angel's feet, in the foreground, lie two guards become 'as

RIGHT: *The Crucifixion (7) from the Passion and Resurrection window. The Cross is shown coloured green, the colour of life bestowed by Christ's blood.*

RIGHT: *The Deposition (8) from the Passion and Resurrection window. Joseph of Arimathea, supporting the body of Christ, and Nicodemus, pulling the nails from His feet, both wear the conical caps symbolizing their Jewishness.*

dead men' (Matt. 28:4). The angel said, 'Go quickly and tell His disciples that He is risen from the dead.'

Magdalene (11), with yellow halo and raised hand, announces the news of Christ's Resurrection to the apostles, led by Peter, shown with a tonsure. Their facial expressions and raised hands suggest amazement and disbelief.

The last three scenes of this window show Jesus physically resurrected. First (12), He appears, holding a book, before two women. One of them, to the left, admires Him with parted hands, whilst the other, upon her knees, reaches for His feet. Jesus's arm movement, and the trees to either side, suggest that this scene principally represents Christ's apparition to Mary Magdalene in the garden, when He said, 'Touch me not [delay me not, or attach yourself not to me], for I am not yet ascended to my Father' (John 20:17).

Finally, just as Jesus appeared to Mary Magdalene as a gardener, so, in the last two scenes of this window, He manifests Himself to two disciples on the road between Jericho and Jerusalem, as a pilgrim, probably because the word 'stranger' used by Cleopas (Luke 24:18), one of the disciples, was a synonym in the Middle Ages for pilgrim.

In the left panel (13), Jesus meets the two disciples, like Himself bare-footed and carrying pilgrims' staffs, walking to Emmaus. The turreted, walled cities to either side of them represent Jericho and Jerusalem. Jesus 'expounded unto them in all the Scriptures the things concerning himself', but they only recognize Him, with expressions of amazement, when, after some time at a meal in Emmaus (14), and before vanishing, He once more, with raised right hand as at the Last Supper, blesses the bread.

THE BLUE VIRGIN WINDOW

In the south ambulatory, set in a 13th-century window restored in 1993, are four more panels of mid 12th-century glass, in which Mary is represented seated frontally, crowned and enthroned, the Child Jesus upon her knee, with angels supporting her celestial throne. Mary's halo and clothing are of luminous blue, set against a rich ruby background. These panels were later incorporated into the present early 13th-century window. Censing angels were added on either side of Mary and, beneath her throne, six scenes narrate the miracle of the changing of water into wine at the marriage feast of Cana, which her Son performed at her request, and at the bottom of the window are shown the three temptations of Christ.

LEFT: *Notre-Dame de la Belle Verrière, or the Blue Virgin, mid 12th century.*

ABOVE: *'Man shall not live by bread alone.' The first temptation of Christ, an early 13th-century panel beneath the Blue Virgin.*

THE 13th CENTURY

THE NORTH PORCH

RIGHT: *The Visitation of Mary (left) to her cousin Elizabeth, North Porch, left bay.*

The six bays of the North and South Porches, constructed mostly between 1200 and 1225, the three great rose windows and more than 150 other lancet or oculus windows, assembled and mounted largely before 1230, constitute by far the most complete of the surviving medieval monumental iconographic programmes. If the architecture is compared to the binding of a book, then its encyclopaedic text is written in stained glass and in sculpture.

This text begins with the story of Paradise Lost, the fault of Adam and Eve, sculpted in the outer archivolts of the central bay of the North Porch, and then narrates the history of humanity from the beginning of the world to the end, with Jesus Christ standing at the centre of time. Those going before Him in the Old Testament prepare for His first coming, as God incarnate; those following behind Him – the saints whose lives exemplify the virtues needed in this world in order to enter the next – prepare for His second coming, as judge, when the worthy may triumph upon time and death and have eternal life in Paradise Regained.

Because Christ said, 'I am the light of the world', there was a medieval tradition (made more complex at Chartres, however) to put the Old Testament figures and narratives on the north, which is the dark side of the church. St Augustine argued that the Old Testament is but the New Testament veiled, and the New Testament is the Old unveiled.

In the North Porch Christ and His Church are prophesied, prepared for and prefigured. Mary is the instrument whereby the prophecies were fulfilled,

BELOW RIGHT: *The death, Assumption and coronation of Mary. North Porch, central bay.*

PREVIOUS PAGE: *The South Rose and South Porch seen from the Tertre de la Poissonnerie.*

FAR RIGHT: *The Judgement of Solomon (on the lintel) and, above, the penance of Job upon his dung-heap. North Porch, right bay.*

and is herself a personification of Ecclesia, the Church, Christ's bride.

The central figures, sculpted on the trumeau, Joachim, Mary's father (vandalized), and St Anne, carrying her child Mary, refer to the apocryphal narratives of Mary's birth, as the three scenes sculpted over the central door concern her death and Assumption, the subject to which Chartres Cathedral is consecrated. On the left part of the lintel Mary reclines, her Son's apostles grouped around her, one feeling her heart, and Christ holding her soul upon His arm. To the right, on the third day, angels lift her body gently from her sepulchre into Heaven, where, in the tympanum, she is seated crowned as Queen of Heaven, reigning eternally on the right hand of her Son and interceding for humanity, but on a slightly lower throne and with a smaller foot stool than Christ. They are surrounded in the five archivolts by angels, Old Testament prophets, and kings and queens of Judah, indicating Mary's double role, celestial and terrestrial, mother of Christ, God and man.

The jamb figures beneath are in chronological order from left to right, from Melchizedek, priest-king, with a chalice containing bread and wine, to Peter, facing him, whose chalice (broken) contains Christ's blood and flesh through His sacrifice, which is the subject prefigured, prophesied and symbolized by the intervening figures. Next to Melchizedek stands Abraham, a protective paternal hand beneath the chin of his son Isaac whom he is prepared to sacrifice, as Christ will be sacrificed by His father. The ram caught in a thicket beneath Isaac's tied feet, as the object sacrificed, is a symbol for Christ. Moses, the law-giver, points to the brazen serpent, with which he healed those bitten by poisonous snakes during the plague of serpents, as Christ will heal humanity's spiritual wounds upon the cross (John 3:14). Aaron (or Samuel) kills a lamb, the most common of the animal symbols representing the sacrifice of Christ, the Lamb of God. King David, especially in Psalm 22, prophesied Christ's Passion and here carries a spear and the crown of thorns. Facing David is the prophet Isaiah, who foretold that 'there shall come forth a rod out of the stem of Jesse', David's father, who reclines on the pedestal. Next comes Jeremiah who, as prophet of Christ's Passion, carries a cross. Simeon, the Christ Child upon his arm, told Mary of the sorrow to come, saying, 'A sword shall pierce through thine own soul also.' John the Baptist is emaciated from fasting in the desert, with drooping, weary shoulders, drawn, haggard features, camel-hair clothing, bare feet crushing a dragon (a symbol of satanic forces), and elongated fingers pointing to the Agnus Dei, the sacrifice of his cousin upon the cross held in

ABOVE: *The North Porch, early 13th century.*

45

BELOW: *Potiphar's wife listening eagerly to the evil counsel of a dragon demon, on the pedestal beneath Joseph. North Porch, right bay.*

ABOVE: *A dog, the traditional symbol of fidelity, sculpted on the pedestal beneath Judith. Although she gave herself to Holofernes to save her people, Judith nevertheless remained faithful to her husband, Manasseh. North Porch, right bay.*

the lamb's paw. The oriflamme fluttering upon the cross symbolizes Christ's victory over death. Peter, on whom Christ built His Church, stands upon a rock, wearing a twelve-stone pectoral to symbolize his inherited priesthood, and carries the keys given to him by Christ to bind and loosen, prefigured by Elijah (on the right) when he passed down his mantle, as he ascended to heaven, to Elisha.

In each of the lateral bays of the North Porch there are six jamb figures, in groups of three. In the right bay, the left figure is Balaam, standing upon his she-ass. He prophesied that a star would rise out of Jacob (Num. 24:17) which, according to the Venerable Bede, means that the Church will rise from Christ. Facing him is one of Jacob's sons, Joseph, a Christ prefiguration, betrayed, exiled in Egypt, and forgiving, with Potiphar's wife on the pedestal eagerly listening to the evil counsel of a demon. The Queen of Sheba and Judith, the central figures on either side, are both prototypes for the Church. Judith saved and protected her people by giving herself to Holofernes, and Sheba has come to listen to the wisdom of Solomon, a Christ figure in his wisdom, as the Church gives the wisdom of Christ. Sheba's visit to Solomon, her negroid servant on the pedestal bringing gifts, also typifies, according to the Church Fathers, the Adoration of

RIGHT *(from left to right): Stripping flax and carding. Scenes of 'active life' from the left bay of the North Porch. February warming his feet by a fire; March trimming the vine; June with a scythe. Three of the monthly labours from the right bay of the North Porch.*

RIGHT: *John the Baptist, holding a disc upon which is sculpted the Agnus Dei, with an oriflammed cross in its paw. North Porch, central bay.*

LEFT: *Figures from the central bay of the North Porch, right jamb. From left to right: Isaiah, Jeremiah, Simeon with the Christ Child, John the Baptist with the Agnus Dei, and Peter, who carries keys and a chalice (broken) and wears a pectoral with 12 stones.*

the Magi. As builder of the temple, Solomon prefigures Christ, builder of the Church, and faces Jesus ben Sirach, to whom medieval theologians attributed both the rebuilding of Solomon's temple (the pedestal scene) and the authorship of the apocryphal book Ecclesiasticus. Solomon prefigures Christ in a third way, as judge on the lintel, and the two mothers claiming a child also typify (according to St Augustine) Ecclesia and the Synagogue, the true and false mothers of humanity. Above, in the tympanum, the patient suffering of Job upon his dung-heap prefigures both Christ's suffering patiently and undeservedly upon the cross and the sufferings of the persecuted Church, His body, an idea expressed by St Gregory and by Pierre de Roissy, chancellor of the Chartres Cathedral School from 1208 to 1213.

In the left bay, the outer figures with scrolls are probably Isaiah and Daniel, prophets of the Incarnation, flanking the Annunciation and Visitation. In each case the figures are turned towards each other, with Mary the inner statue, to the left trampling upon the serpent and to the right standing upon the burning bush, a symbol for her unconsumed virginity. Upon the lintel are the Nativity and the Annunciation to the Shepherds, and on the tympanum is sculpted the Adoration of the Magi, bringing their gifts to acknowledge that Jesus is man, king and God.

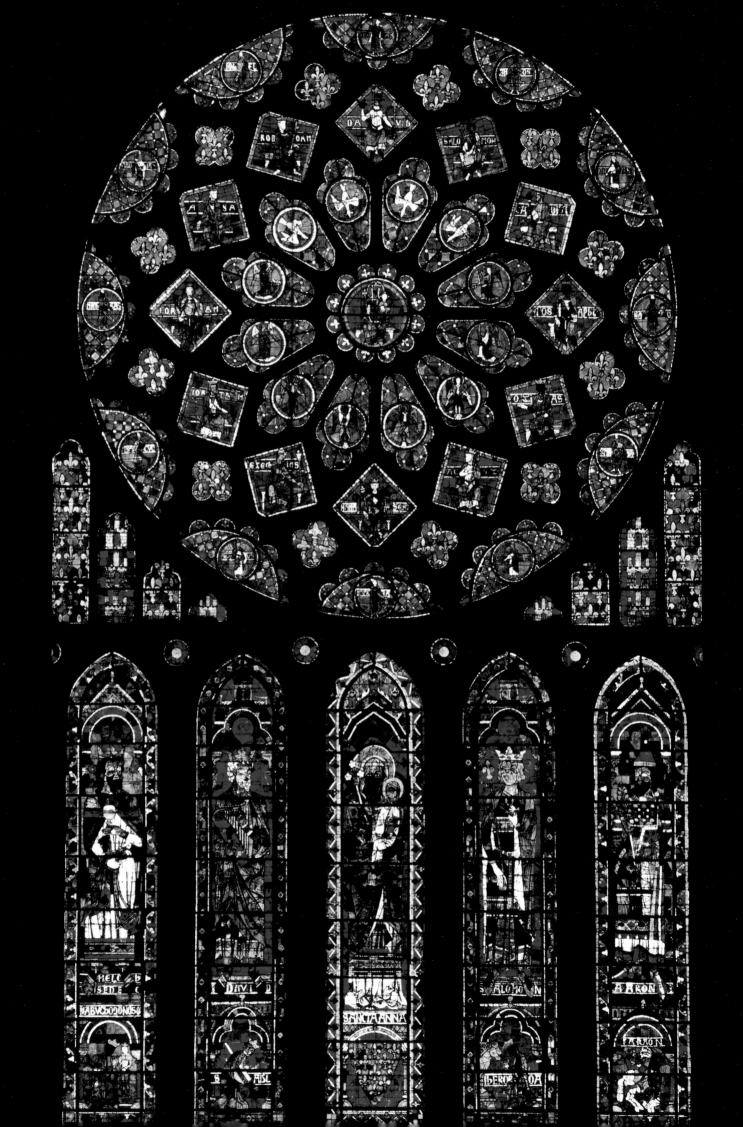

THE NORTH ROSE WINDOW

The North Rose and lancets, about 1230 and given by Queen Blanche of Castile, repeat the two principal themes of the North Porch; the Old Testament figures prophesy or prefigure Christ, and Mary is the instrument whereby the prophecies were fulfilled. The twelve minor prophets in the outer semicircles agreed with the four major prophets beneath the South Rose opposite, that the Christ should come from the royal House of David. In the squares are twelve kings of Judah, Christ's ancestors, with four doves and eight angels surrounding Mary and Child. Beneath the rose the central figure, as in the North Porch, is St Anne with the child Mary whom, according to the apocryphal writings, she conceived immaculately. To either side of Anne, in each of the other four windows, are two Old Testament figures, the large ones prefiguring Christ as priests and kings (christos = the anointed one), trampling underfoot smaller figures, anti-christs. On the extreme left stands the doubly anointed priest-king Melchizedek, carrying a chalice and representing the virtue of faith, with the vice of idolatry beneath in the form of King Nebuchadnezzar. Next comes David, with his ten-stringed harp. Like Christ, David was a new king of the Jews, anointed by Samuel after defeating King Saul, who is shown beneath committing suicide, the traditional way of depicting despair. As a forebear of Christ, David represents hope for humanity. His son Solomon, to the right of Anne, prefigures Christ as judge, as builder of the temple, and in his wisdom. Beneath him the mad King Jeroboam, another idolator, worships golden calves. On the extreme right the high priest Aaron wears the Jewish ephod and carries the flowering rod given to him by Moses, while his persecutor, Pharaoh, like Pride, falls head first from his horse into the Red Sea.

BELOW LEFT: *King Jeroboam worshipping two golden calves. Detail from a lancet beneath the North Rose.*

BELOW RIGHT: *King Saul. Detail from a lancet beneath the North Rose window.*

LEFT: *The North Rose window, about 1230, given by Queen Blanche of Castile, whose coats of arms decorate the spandrels. The figures in the five lancet windows are Melchizedek and Nebuchadnezzar, David and Saul, St Anne, Solomon and Jeroboam, and Aaron and his persecutor the Pharaoh, who is falling into the Red Sea. The rose window is composed of 12 semicircles containing the 12 minor prophets and 12 squares with 12 kings of Judah; doves and angels surround the central figure of the Virgin and Child.*

49

THE SYMBOLIC WINDOW OF THE REDEMPTION

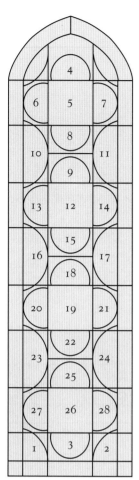

At the base of the window are the donors – the farriers – shown in three scenes, stoking a furnace (1), hammering upon an anvil (2) and shoeing a horse, placed within a wooden frame and held firmly by its bridle and hind leg (3).

Unfortunately, probably in 1816, a falling gutter damaged seven of the central panels in the upper half (4, 5, 8, 9, 12, 15 and 18), and it was decided not to restore but to replace them with plain glass. The present panels, copies of the originals, were made in 1876 but not mounted until 1923.

This window is one of the most richly symbolic at Chartres and is similar to others in the cathedrals of Bourges, Canterbury, Rouen, Lyon, Le Mans and Tours, all of which illustrate the medieval belief in the concordance of the two testaments. Old Testament scenes are grouped around other panels that narrate the Passion of Jesus Christ.

In the uppermost panel, He is enthroned (4), blessing, between two three-branched candlesticks, above the first scene of His Passion (5), in which He is shown carrying a green cross. To the left (6) are weeping women, and to the right (7) Roman soldiers, one with a ladder to nail Him on the cross.

Beneath (8), is the first Old Testament prefiguration. Two of the twelve spies sent out by Moses (Num. 13:24) to find the Promised Land return from Eschol bearing a huge bunch of grapes upon a staff. According to Isidore of Seville, quoted in the *Glossa ordinaria*, the grapes suspended on a pole symbolize Christ hanging on the cross, for He is the mystic grape whose blood fills the chalice of the Church. The two spies personify the Jews and the Gentiles, for he who leads (in representations elsewhere sometimes even shown wearing a Jewish conical cap) turns his back upon the grapes, as the Jews disregard Christ, whilst he who follows behind, his eyes fixed upon the grapes, as at Canterbury, personifies the Gentiles who followed Christ.

A similar interpretation was given to the double miracle of Gideon's fleece, in the next panel down (9), although it is not certain that this was the subject of the original panel. Gideon is shown threshing wheat, when an angel appeared to him and told him to deliver Israel from the Midinites. At Gideon's request for heavenly signs, his fleece at first was bedewed and the surrounding ground left dry, and in the second miracle the reverse happened. The first miracle symbolizes God's blessing of the Jewish nation, and the second his favouring the Gentiles, who accepted Jesus as the Christ, rejected by the Jews.

Then come three more scenes from Christ's Passion. He is crowned with green thorns (10), tied to a stake and scourged (11), then crucified (12) upon a green cross. A soldier pierces His right side

RIGHT: *The Redemption window. A typological window in which six scenes illustrating Christ's Passion are surrounded by Old Testament prefigurations of both His death and Resurrection.*

with a lance, whilst another mockingly offers a sponge soaked in vinegar. Mary and John stand by, grief-stricken.

The two female figures to either side of the Crucifixion personify the Church and the Synagogue. On Christ's right (our left) is Ecclesia (13), represented as a saint and queen, with nimbus and crown, holding a cruciform standard in one hand and a miniature church in the other. The woman to His left allegorizes the Synagogue (14), with broken banner and toppling crown, for she has been dethroned by Ecclesia. A serpent is entwined about her head and, to emphasize her blindness further, a small demon shoots an arrow through her eyes.

Kneeling at the foot of the cross is Adam (15), wearing a shroud and holding a chalice to receive Christ's redeeming blood. It was believed in the Middle Ages that the cross was made from the wood of the Tree of Life that had grown in the Garden of Eden, and that Adam was buried at Golgotha (place of the skull), where Jesus died. As Mary is the second Eve, so Christ is the second Adam, 'for as in Adam all die, even so in Christ shall all be made alive' (1 Cor. 15:22).

Moses (16), holding the tablets of the law, is represented traditionally with horns that project from his head, the result of a mistranslation into Latin of a Hebrew word that really meant rays (Exod. 34:29). As in the North Porch, he is lifting up the brass serpent, a strange dragon-like creature upon a column, to heal those bitten by poisonous snakes (Num. 21:6–9). Later, John wrote: 'As Moses lifted up the brass serpent in the wilderness, even so must the Son of Man be lifted up' – on the cross to heal humanity's spiritual wounds.

Opposite (17) is yet another Old Testament scene interpreted as referring to the cross and Christ's sacrifice. An Israelite is marking the lintel of his house with the mysterious sign of the tau (T), which resembles a cross. It is made with the blood of a lamb, Christ symbolized, the Lamb of God.

Between these two scenes is the last of the 19th-century panels, but the first of a series that deal with the theme of resurrection. Jonah (18), vomited from the sea-monster's belly on the third day, was one of the most popular of the Old Testament subjects understood to prefigure Christ's Resurrection, 'for as Jonah was three days and three nights in the whale's belly, so shall the Son of Man be three days and three nights in the heart of the earth' (Matt. 12:40).

The lower half of this window dates from the 13th century and represents two more scenes from Christ's Passion (in the squares), surrounded by more Old Testament prefigurations. First is the Deposition (19). Joseph of Arimathea lifts Jesus's limp body from the cross. John stands to one side

LEFT: *Abraham with knife and torch prepares to sacrifice his son Isaac (20), who carries the wood for his sacrifice, like Jesus, in the form of a green cross. Detail from the Redemption window.*

and Mary to the other kissing her Son's hand, whilst Nicodemus, kneeling and in white, detaches His feet from the suppedaneum to which they are nailed. In the semicircles on either side of the Deposition, Abraham prepares to sacrifice his son Isaac. According to the *Glossa ordinaria*, Abraham is a figure for God the Father, and Isaac prefigures God the Son. In other windows at Bourges and Canterbury, in fact, Isaac is even depicted carrying a cross, whilst here he carries the sticks for his sacrifice tied in two bundles, crossed so that the symbolism is implied (20). Opposite (21), Isaac is laid upon an altar and Abraham is about to slay him, but his arm is stayed by an angel pointing to a ram caught by its horns in a thicket which he is to sacrifice instead. The ram is a symbol for Christ the sacrifice, the thicket represents the cross, and its thorns refer to those with which Jesus was crowned.

In the semicircle beneath the Deposition (22), David sits with a pelican. In Psalm 22, which begins 'My God, why hast thou forsaken me?' and mentions the piercing of hands and feet, David foretold Christ's Passion. On his scroll is written 'similis factus sum pellicamo' (I am like the pelican). According to Honorius of Autun, the pelican (believed to kill its young and to resurrect them upon the third day with its blood) symbolizes both

ABOVE: *David seated with a pelican, resurrecting her chicks with her own blood (22). Detail from the Redemption window. North aisle.*

God the Father, who resurrected his Son on the third day, and Christ on the cross, whose blood resurrects mortal humanity. A similar interpretation was given to the Shunamite woman's dead son, resurrected by Elisha (23), where again the resurrection prefigured is that of mankind through Christ, rather than that of Christ Himself. In the panel opposite (24), the prophet Elijah, traditionally bald, holds a scroll upon which is written 'Elias Profeta'. Persecuted by the Jews, he fled into Zidon and came to Zarephath, where he met a widow gathering sticks (shown in the form of a cross), and asked her for water. Elijah prefigures Christ, rejected by the Synagogue, and the widow of Zarephath personifies the Church, welcoming him; the water she has drawn shows her belief in the virtue of baptism, and the sticks show that she looks to the cross for salvation.

Between Elisha and Elijah is another symbolic scene (25), again interpreted, especially by Isidore of Seville, as referring to the cross. The patriarch Jacob, seated, blesses his two grandsons, Ephraim and Manasseh, but with crossed arms, so that the right hand is placed upon the head of the younger of the brothers, Ephraim. Jacob's blessing was interpreted as typifying the New Covenant, the Jews

being represented by Manasseh and the Gentiles by Ephraim.

In the lowest square (26) is the last of the six scenes that narrate Christ's Passion, the Anointing and Entombment. Joseph of Arimathea and Nicodemus the Pharisee lower His body into a sarcophagus, whilst a third person pours oil from a phial. Two other figures with haloes, in attitudes of grief, are probably Mary and John the Apostle.

To the left (27) another Old Testament narrative prefigures both Christ's Resurrection and Ascension. Samson came to Gaza, and the Philistines, believing that they might capture him, locked the city gates, but 'Samson rose at midnight, and took the doors of the gate of the city . . . and put them on his shoulders, and carried them up on to the top of a hill' (Judg. 16:3) – like the sticks of Isaac, shown in the form of a cross – just as Jesus broke out of His sepulchre, and ascended to demonstrate that He had overcome death.

In the final scene to the right of the Entombment, the boy David (28) protects his sheep by slaying a lion which, according to St Augustine and Adam of St Victor, symbolizes Christ's defeat of Satan through His triumph over death on the cross, thereby protecting His father's people.

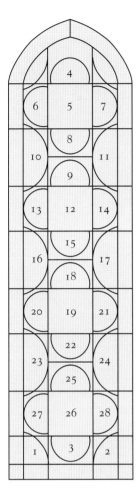

RIGHT: *Samson, carrying off the gates of Gaza up onto the mountain (27), prefigures Christ's Resurrection and Ascension. Detail from the Redemption window. North aisle.*

THE JOSEPH WINDOW

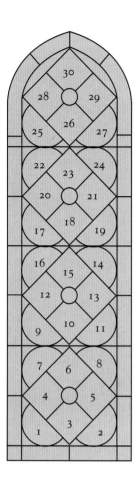

RIGHT: *The Joseph window*.

The donors (1 and 2), money-changers, are shown at the base of the window behind a green bench upon which are coins and scales. In medieval Chartres they set up their benches to the south of the cathedral in the street still called Rue des Changes.

Joseph prefigures Christ in many ways. His life, therefore, as narrated here and in a similar window at Bourges, should be read typologically. The sources of inspiration were probably to some extent the Biblical commentaries of Isidore of Seville, but again especially the popular *Glossa ordinaria*. Thus Joseph's dream (3), in which the sun, moon and stars make obeisance to him (Gen. 37:9), refers also to Christ, for it was foretold of Him that 'the sun, moon and stars will adore thee'. Similarly, Jacob sending Joseph (4) with a green jug of water and three loaves to his brothers in the fields of Shechem prefigures Jesus sent by His father to his brethren on earth, and both were betrayed. With heads grouped conspiratorially (5), Joseph's brothers plotted against him and decided to slay him. Reuben, the eldest brother, suggested that they thrust him into a pit (6), which typifies Christ's descent to Hell for three days. Ishmeelite merchants passed by (7), and Judah said 'Let us sell him', and he was sold for twenty pieces of silver, as Jesus was sold by Judas for thirty. Joseph's brothers took the many-coloured coat back to Jacob (8), tinged in the blood of a wild beast. The many-coloured coat symbolizes Christ's human form, given to Him by His father, and taken off Him, blood-stained, on the cross.

The following scenes take place in Egypt, where Joseph, again like Jesus, was exiled, and sold to Potiphar (9), whose wife tried to tempt him (10), but he recoiled in horror and ran away, leaving his cloak, which was then taken to Potiphar (11). Like the many-coloured coat, the cloak was interpreted as another symbol for Christ's human form, left behind on the cross.

Having been falsely accused (12), Joseph was taken and thrust into prison (13) with Pharaoh's butler and chief cook, as Jesus was crucified between two thieves. In prison (14), the butler, to the left, dreamed that he pressed grapes into a cup which he offered to Pharaoh and, to the right, the baker, sleeping, saw a basket with bread eaten by a bird, which Joseph interpreted as meaning that the butler would be released from prison but the baker hanged after three days, just as one of the thieves crucified with Jesus was saved while the other was damned.

Two years later, Pharaoh dreamed (15) of the seven fat kine eaten by the seven lean ones (16). Joseph was brought out of prison and, kneeling before Pharaoh seated upon a throne (17), inter-

preted his dream, saying: 'Behold there come seven years of great plenty throughout all the land of Egypt, and there shall arise after them seven years of famine.' The Egyptians, in the next two scenes, sow (18) and store grain (19) in readiness for the famine.

Jacob, seated and bearded (20), also suffered from the great famine and sent his sons, here astride dromedaries (21), to buy grain. Joseph, sceptre in hand as lord of Egypt, accompanied by two attendants (22), greeted them, 'but they knew him not'.

The window does not relate the episode of the brothers' return to Canaan to bring Benjamin to Egypt, but when they returned with Benjamin, Joseph entertained them (23), 'and they drank, and were merry with him'. Their sacks were filled with grain, but a silver cup was concealed in that of Benjamin. Joseph's steward then arrested the brothers, and Benjamin is seen expressing his astonishment when the cup is found in his sack (24).

Having wept and revealed himself as their brother, Joseph sent for his father, who greeted his sons (25), again astride dromedaries, which have small bells around their necks (26 and 27).

Accompanied by his sons, Jacob then set out on horseback for Egypt (28), where he was reunited with Joseph (29), 'who fell upon his neck, and wept a good while'.

At the top of the window is Jesus (30) who, like Joseph, triumphed over His sufferings, forgave His betrayers and was reunited with His father.

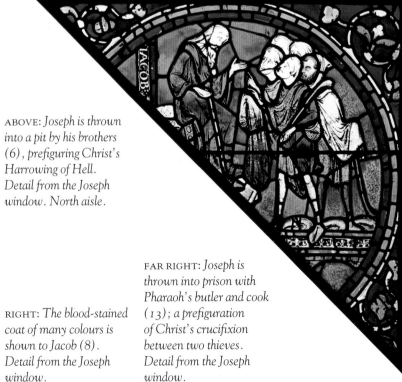

ABOVE: *Joseph is thrown into a pit by his brothers (6), prefiguring Christ's Harrowing of Hell. Detail from the Joseph window. North aisle.*

FAR RIGHT: *Joseph is thrown into prison with Pharaoh's butler and cook (13); a prefiguration of Christ's crucifixion between two thieves. Detail from the Joseph window.*

RIGHT: *The blood-stained coat of many colours is shown to Jacob (8). Detail from the Joseph window.*

THE NOAH WINDOW

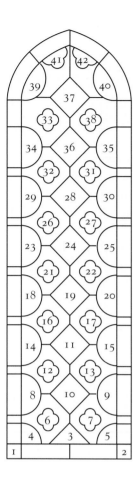

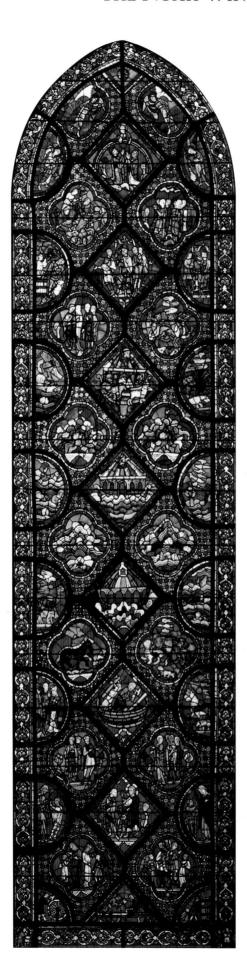

RIGHT: *The Noah window, about 1210.*

Appropriately, the Noah window was donated by coopers (1 and 5), carpenters with various tools (2) and stripping the bark off a log (3), and wheelwrights (4); for Noah, as builder of the ark, was patron of carpenters and, as the first planter of a vineyard, patron of coopers (and, incidentally, drunkards!).

According to early medieval writers, including once more Isidore of Seville (*Allegoriae quaedam scripturae sacrae*), Noah as saviour is another Christ prefiguration, and the ark, as the means of saving, is a symbol for the Church. Thus the flood symbolizes both baptism – cleansing through water – and the Last Judgement.

In four curious scenes (6, 7, 8 and 9), at the base of the window, difficult to identify, tall figures apparently converse with smaller people, some with shepherds' crooks, others armed with clubs and even a blood-stained lance. The reference, perhaps, is to prediluvian times, when 'there were giants in the earth . . . and also after that, when the sons of God came in unto the daughters of men, and they bare children to them, the same became mighty men . . . and the earth was filled with violence, and God looked upon the earth, and beheld it was corrupt . . . and God said unto Noah (10), 'The end of all flesh is come before me . . . make thee an ark' (Gen. 6:4,11–14). Helped perhaps by one of his sons, Noah built an ark (11), surrounded by members of his family (12, 13, 14), for God had bidden him bring 'thou, and thy sons, and thy wife and thy sons' wives with thee. And of every living thing of all flesh, two of every sort.' A procession in pairs of sheep, horses, swine and fowl (15), elephants, lions and camels (16, 17, 18) prepares to enter the ark before the flood.

'And it came to pass after seven days that the waters of the flood were upon the earth.' Floating on turbulent waters, the ark is represented like a church (19), with masonry, columns with capitals, and arches. The ark and the flood being symbols for the Church and the Last Judgement respectively, the drowned (20, 21, 22, 23, 26 and 27) then prefigure the damned.

After forty days, Noah opened the window of the ark, and sent forth a raven, here shown devouring a floating corpse (29). 'He also sent forth a dove' (24), and seven days later, the waters having receded and the trees reappeared (25), the dove, released a second time, returned, 'and, lo, in her mouth was an olive leaf plucked off'. Both olive branch and dove symbolize peace. Noah and his

LEFT: *Noah, assisted by one of his sons, builds the ark (11).*

family and 'every living thing of all flesh' left the ark (28, 30 and 31) and God, surrounded by censing angels (39, 40, 41 and 42), reconciled with his people, proclaimed: 'I do set my bow in the cloud (37), and it shall be for a token of a covenant between me and the earth.' Noah and his wife are shown kneeling beneath the rainbow (37).

Before this final scene, however, the window illustrates another brief narrative from Genesis 9. Noah, accompanied by a man and two women (32), discovers the vine, which is cultivated (33). Grapes are gathered, trodden, and wine poured (34) and

LEFT: *The flood and the drowned, with Noah releasing a dove in the central square (24). To the right the dove is returning with an olive twig in its beak. Detail from the Noah window.*

ABOVE: *Two by two the animals, elephants, lions, birds, arrive to embark (17).*

BELOW: *Noah and his wife kneel beneath the rainbow (37).*

served to Noah (35), whose ensuing drunkenness is not shown, but, having been derided by his youngest son, Ham, he cursed him (36) so that his offspring would be servants to those of his brothers.

The other three north aisle windows narrate the lives of saints. Next to Noah is St Lubin (**63**), a 6th-century bishop of Chartres who was invoked against dropsy and was patron saint of the donors – inn-keepers and wine-merchants – two reasons, perhaps, for placing him next to Noah.

To the left of Joseph is the life of St Eustace (**62**) who, like Joseph, was exiled in Egypt, suffered great misfortunes, was separated from his family and reunited with them. To the right of Joseph is the life of St Nicholas (**60**), one of whose miracles was to produce wheat during a famine. Furriers donated the St Eustace window, for his history begins with a hunt (seen in the lowest panel). Grocers and haberdashers gave the St Nicholas window because he was their patron.

THE JOHN THE DIVINE WINDOW

RIGHT: *John sits in his grave, awaiting his ascension (16). Detail from the John the Divine window.*

BELOW: *Details from the complex arrangement of the St John window. In the lower panel (13) John is challenged by the seated High Priest of Diana to drink poison. In the upper panel (14) he does so, surviving under the protecting hand of God, while the faithless die.*

The mid 12th-century west lancets having narrated Christ's birth, death and Resurrection, (see pages 30 to 40) five of the six south aisle windows concern events in the lives of those closest to Him: John the Divine, Mary Magdalene and His mother. Their subject-matter, however, was largely taken from non-Biblical sources, whilst another window in this group, which combines the parable of the Good Samaritan with the story of Adam and Eve, although Biblical, was inspired more by the commentaries of the early Church Fathers.

With the exception of the Vendôme Chapel window (**8**) with its four lights and flamboyant tracery, given by Louis de Bourbon, Count of Vendôme, in about 1417, the other five south aisle windows, like the north ones, date from about 1210, and were given by more merchant brotherhoods.

Because St John, according to legend, was thrown into a cauldron of boiling oil from which he emerged unharmed at the Latin Gate when he came to Rome, he was the patron of armourers, the donors of this window. Unfortunately, one of their 'signatures' has been missing since at least the 17th century, and was replaced by a fragment (1), representing a flight into Egypt, that obviously does not belong to this window. In two other panels, however, the donors are shown, to the left (2) fashioning a shield, and to the right (3), at their forge making stirrups with hammer and tongs, file and anvil.

The narrative of this window closely follows the liturgical text for the feast of St John, December 27, and tells of the saint's exile on Patmos, and his last years at Ephesus, where he lived until a great age.

During the reigns of Nero and Domitian Christians were persecuted and John, aboard a boat (4) sought exile on Patmos, where he is then represented seated (5), writing the book of the Revelation. Around him are seven aedicules, which symbolize the seven churches of Asia to which the book is addressed (Rev. 1:4 and 11).

When Domitian died, John went to Ephesus, and at the city gate came upon the funeral procession of Drusiana, who had so ardently desired his return, and John ordered the bier to be placed on the ground, and the bandages to be unwrapped, and said, 'Drusiana, my Lord Jesus Christ resurrects you. Arise, go to your house and prepare me a meal. Sitting up (6), like Lazarus in the next window, still wearing her funeral shroud, she reaches out towards John, who blesses her, whilst bystanders (7) proclaim, 'The God of whom John speaks is the one God, Jesus Christ is the only true God.'

Next day, John came upon a philosopher, named Craton, preaching renunciation (8). Two young disciples of his, having sold their goods and converted them into precious stones, are shown smashing them with hammers. John admonished them, saying, 'if thou wilt be perfect, sell all that thou hast and give to the poor', whereupon Craton bade John, if his master be the true God, make the stones whole again. John (9) standing, blesses with one hand, and holds the restored jewels in the other, whilst Craton and his disciples express their astonishment.

Two other young men, Atticus and Eugenius, impressed by John's miracle, then sold their goods, gave all to the poor, and followed the apostle. John, perceiving that the youths regretted their former wealth, one day picked up wood and pebbles on the beach and converted them to gold and precious stones, and told them to go back and buy back their lands, 'for you have lost the grace of God. Be sumptuously dressed that you may be beggared for eternity.' Two panels in this window show first John (10) with the two young men, one holding sticks turning to gold, the other a platter of gems. Then in a second (11) the golden rods are presented to a money-changer, seated (as in the Joseph window) at a coin-covered bench.

Meanwhile a newly wed youth, Stactus, died (12). A tiny red demon seizes his soul; his wife in the foreground and others behind, mourn. Strangely, it is this scene which is shown, and not that of his resurrection when John bade him explain to Atticus and Eugenius the joys of Heaven and the torments of Hell.

Next comes one of the most popular of all the Johannine legends, that of the poisoned cup. The high priest of Diana at Ephesus, named Aristodemus (13), seated with another fearsome character beside him, told John that he would believe in his God if he would drink the poison he gave him. Reptiles are crushed into a jar, and two condemned men forced to drink the poison lie dead (14). John swallows the poison but the divine hand above him symbolizes his miraculous immunity, for Christ had promised the apostles, if they drink any deadly thing, it shall not hurt them (Mk. 16:18).

The remaining five panels narrate the legend of John's ascension. Christ (15) appeared to John aged 99, and said, 'It is time that thou satest with thy brethren at my table.' The following Sunday, the apostle caused a grave to be dug, here represented as a sarcophagus supported by pillars, in which he is sitting, hands joined in prayer. A great blinding light came, in which he vanished, and those present bent over the grave, and found it filled with sweet-smelling manna. Censing angels (17 and 18) with outstretched arms (19) welcome John, like Enoch and Elijah, Jesus and Mary, bodily ascended into the Kingdom of Heaven.

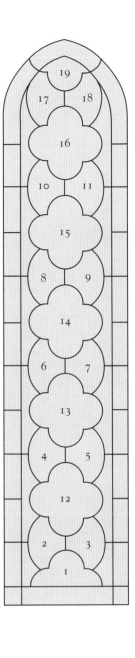

LEFT: *St John the Divine window, about 1210. South aisle.*

THE MARY MAGDALENE WINDOW

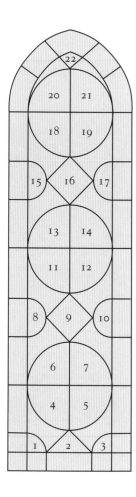

RIGHT: *The Mary Magdalene window, about 1210.*

The three figures emptying jugs at the base of this window are the donors, water-carriers (1, 2 and 3). Mary of Magdala, whom Jesus had healed of seven devils, was one of the women who followed Him in Galilee, was present at His crucifixion, came to His tomb and found it empty. According to St Mark, it was to her that Jesus first appeared and, according to St John, gave the message to take to His apostles that He was resurrected.

Medieval Western theologians, following St Gregory the Great, considered Mary of Magdala, Mary of Bethany (the sister of Martha and Lazarus) and the 'woman who was a sinner' spoken of by St Luke, as the same person, whereas the Eastern theologians believed them to be three separate women. Thus in the Western Church Mary of Magdala typifies the repentant sinner. She first met Jesus at the house of Simon the Pharisee (4). Jesus, with cruciform nimbus, is seated at a table on the far left, with Simon beside Him and two other unidentified guests. Mary Magdalene, kneeling before Him, a box of ointments beside her, 'began to wash His feet with tears, and did wipe them with the hairs of her head, and kissed His feet, and anointed them with the ointment . . . and He said to her, thy sins are forgiven . . . go in peace'.

The next six scenes illustrate the miracle of the raising of Lazarus. In the first (5), he is laid out, covered with a blue shroud. Three funerary candles stand beside his death-bed. Mary Magdalene and Martha are comforted by two Jews. Then he is placed in a red sepulchre (6 and 7), whilst his sisters and two other figures, one hooded, the other wearing a Jewish conical cap, look on distressed. A figure wearing bishop's robes officiates, his crozier carried by a cleric with an open book. Four days later, Jesus came to Bethany, and Martha and Mary brought Him to their brother's grave (8); and 'He cried with a loud voice, Lazarus come forth. And he that was dead came forth, bound hand and foot with grave-clothes' (9), whilst bystanders (10) cover their noses, because 'by this time he stanketh'!

Hence, the Magdalene was present at the resurrections both of her brother and of Jesus Christ, narrated in the next three scenes. When she comes to the holy sepulchre, an angel, as in the Passion window, shows her the shroud hanging from the empty tomb (11). It was to the Magdalene that Jesus, holding a cross (12), first appeared, and she at first mistook Him for the gardener. Then, recognizing Him she wished to touch Him, but His attitude expresses His words, 'Delay me not, for I am not yet ascended to my father', and He bade her announce His resurrection to His disciples (13 and 14).

Because of the medieval devotion to Mary Magdalene, many legends became attached to her,

BELOW: *The raising of Lazarus (9). Martha and Mary take Jesus to the grave, Jesus raises Lazarus. Details from the Mary Magdalene window.*

ABOVE: *Mary Magdalene washes Jesus's feet with her tears and dries them with her hair (4). Detail from the Mary Magdalene window.*

and one of the most popular, narrated in the remaining third of this window, tells how, with her brother Lazarus, sister Martha, St Maximin and other Christians, she was put to sea by infidels and abandoned in a boat without sails, oars or pilot. This last fact, however, is not mentioned in the medieval Chartres text which probably inspired the window, for the Magdalene is shown (15) disembarking in Provence from a boat which has sails and even a pilot holding an oar. St Maximin, the future bishop of Aix-en-Provence, shown already with

mitre and crozier, speaks to a group of people (16), probably from the neighbouring city, Marseille (17).

Having become a hermit on the Sainte-Baume, a mountain near Marseille, Mary Magdalene died there (18). A cleric holds a cross near her head, whilst Bishop Maximin reads prayers for the dead from a book supported upon a lectern. The same figures are present at her entombment (19), when her body is lowered into a yellow sepulchre.

In the final scene (20, 21 and 22), an angel dressed in red respectfully presents her soul upon a white napkin to Jesus, who is shown blessing. Three more angels participate, two of them censing, on the far right and in the apex panel; the other, on the far left, holds the crown of life, as the Magdalene, the repentant sinner, is welcomed into the Kingdom of Heaven.

The Good Samaritan and Adam and Eve Window

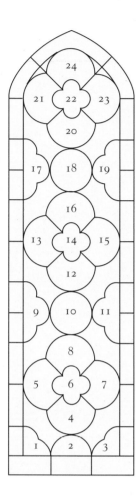

RIGHT: *The Good Samaritan and Adam and Eve window, about 1210.*

The donors, shoe-makers, are shown in the three bottom scenes, at their work (1 and 2), and offering the window to the cathedral with an inscription (3).

This window, like others at Bourges and Sens cathedrals combines the parable of the Good Samaritan with the narrative of the creation and fall of Adam and Eve, thereby illustrating a symbolic interpretation of Christ's parable that was popular in the Middle Ages.

The lower half tells the parable straightforwardly. Two seated figures, one wearing a Jewish bonnet and beneath whom is written 'Fariseus', listen to Jesus, shown with raised hand (4). 'A certain man went down from Jerusalem [a walled city to the left] to Jericho (5), and fell amongst thieves (6 and 7), who stripped him of his raiment, and wounded him leaving him half dead. 'A priest and then a Levite walked by without helping (8). 'But a certain Samaritan, as he journeyed, came where he was . . . and went to him, and bound up his wounds (9) . . . and set him on his own beast (10), and brought him to an inn (11), and took care of him (12), promising to return and settle debts.'

The upper half of the window is composed of scenes from Genesis 2, 3 and 4, which are related to the symbolic interpretation of the parable in the lower half.

God, with Christ's features, created Adam, and 'breathed into his nostrils the breath of life' (13). Beneath them is written 'Creator Hominis'. 'And the Lord God planted a garden eastward of Eden, and there He put the man He had formed' (14), and He 'caused a deep sleep to fall on Adam' (15), during which He created Eve from Adam's side. He then showed Adam and Eve the forbidden fruit of the knowledge of good and evil (16); the tempting serpent is clearly seen, red, entwined around the trunk. Seated beneath the tree, Eve suggests to Adam that they eat of the fruit (17). Having done so (18), Adam is shown choking, hand clutching at his throat, where the apple is stuck (Adam's apple!) 'And the eyes of both of them were opened, and they knew that they were naked . . . and hid themselves amongst the trees of the garden' (19). An angel, brandishing a flaming sword, then expels them from Paradise, represented as a red door (20), and they are condemned to work; Adam is shown delving and Eve spinning (21). The gaining of the knowledge of good and evil resulted in a *psychomachia*, a struggling of the soul, and the satanic forces soon achieved their first victory, when Cain killed his brother Abel (23).

Very early commentaries on Jesus's parable were written by Irenaeus of Lyon (about 180), Clement of Alexandria (about 200) and his pupil Origen.

LEFT: *Part of the Good Samaritan window. Jesus, in the lowest petal of the quatrefoil (right), is teaching the parable (4). Above, left to right, a man is leaving Jerusalem, and is set upon by thieves (5–7). In the upper petal (8), he is left wounded upon the wayside as a priest then a Levite walk past.*

Later, homilies on the same subject were written by Ambrose of Milan and the Venerable Bede, in his *Non oculi scribarum*, but the symbolic interpretation of the parable was known especially through the *Glossa ordinaria*.

Hence, the man leaving Jerusalem represents fallen mankind leaving Paradise. Jerusalem is sometimes used in the Scriptures as a symbolic name for Eden (Salem is an early form of *shalom*, meaning peace), just as Paradise Regained is referred to by the author of the Book of the Revelation as the New or Heavenly Jerusalem. The thieves attacking and stripping the man of his clothes allegorize the temptations that beset mankind, depriving him of his immortality. The priest and Levite represent the Old Testament unable to heal humanity's spiritual wounds. The Samaritan is Christ Himself, the inn symbolizes His Church and the promise to return refers to His second coming to judge the quick and the dead. In the topmost scene (24), seated upon a rainbow between two angels, is Christ, the Samaritan-Redeemer, holding the globe of the world in His left hand and blessing with His right.

BELOW: *God shows Adam and Eve the forbidden fruit (16).*

THE ASSUMPTION WINDOW

The donors, again shoe-makers, are represented in five scenes here. They are working with various tools (1 and 2), selling a shoe to a customer, who is seated, cross-legged, his old boot in his right hand (3), piercing eye-holes for laces (4) and cutting leather (5).

The remainder of this window relates the death, funeral, Assumption and Coronation of Mary, a story which, although apocryphal, was so popular in the late 12th and early 13th centuries that most of the great cathedrals of that period represent one or other of these scenes. Although the dogma of Mary's Assumption was not proclaimed until 1950 by Pope Pius XII, Chartres has been consecrated to it since at least the 13th century.

The earliest text is attributed to Melion, a disciple of St John, or to St John himself. Later it is found in a summarized form in the writings of St Gregory of Tours (*De gloria martyrium*), and again in an 8th-century sermon attributed to St John of Damascus. Evidently the Chartres clergy and the artists of this window knew the story well, even

ABOVE: *Mary's funeral procession (12). Detail from the Assumption window.*

RIGHT: *The Death of Mary (6). Detail from the Assumption window.*

before it was further popularized later in the 13th century by Vincent de Beauvais and by Jacques de Voragine in his *Golden Legend*.

In the first scene (6), Mary reclines upon her death-bed, the apostles grouped around her in attitudes of grief, having been 'ravished by a mysterious force, which brought these together in Mary's room, where she lay awaiting death'. One of them, in blue, is feeling her heart. To the right are two weeping women (7) and to the left (8) another woman shows an unidentified figure the drama taking place in the adjacent panel. The three women are probably the three virgins who, according to the Pseudo-Meliton, washed Mary's corpse before her entombment.

'And about the third hour of the night, Jesus Christ came ... with the orders of the angels, the companies of patriarchs, the assembly of martyrs, the convents of confessors, the carols of virgins', reduced in this window to two symmetrical groups of four figures (10 and 11) to either side of Christ (9) who, with two more angels, receives His mother's soul, represented as a small child, which He blesses and lifts into Heaven.

Mary's funeral follows (12). Her coffin is carried by seven apostles, with Peter, probably, in front, and Paul behind. John, holding the celestial palm, is one of four other apostles on either side in pairs (13 and 14). According to the *Golden Legend*, a Jewish high priest named Jephomias, here shown in red and green, tried to halt the procession and seize the coffin, whereupon his hand withered. Having pleaded with Peter to help, he was told 'to kiss the bier, and say "I believe in Jesus Christ, and in Mary, who bore him in her womb, yet remained virgin"', and then the hand was restored 'all whole perfectly'. Above, to either side, and again symmetrically, groups of four figures (15 and 16), three with haloes, five without, flank censing angels (17), witnessing the funeral procession below.

Gently, held in a shroud, Mary's body is lowered into a blue sarcophagus (18) by the apostles, who then kept watch for three days until her Assumption. On the third day following her death, angels translated her uncorrupted body, contained within an aureole (19), into Heaven, where Jesus (20) crowned her, and sat her upon His right hand, as Solomon crowned his mother, Bathsheba, and she reigned with him on his right hand. Jesus is here represented in the act of crowning His mother, as at Sens and Reims. The Holy Ghost appears in a cloud in the form of a dove, and on either side an angel holds another crown suspended over Mary's head (27). Placed symmetrically in the border scenes, more censing angels (21, 22, 23 and 24) acclaim Mary, the Queen of Heaven, Mother of God, mankind's most powerful intercessor (25, 26).

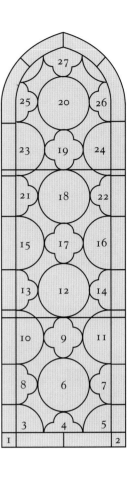

LEFT: *The Assumption window, about 1210.*

THE LIFE OF MARY WINDOW

The remaining lower storey windows in the transept and ambulatory date with a few exceptions from the early 13th century, and form a hagiographical programme, similar to that of the South Porch. The acts of the apostles and the lives of martyrs and confessors illustrate Christ's teaching, thereby offering humanity examples to emulate. With the exception of St James the Greater (**37**), placed next to Charlemagne (**38**), who delivered his tomb from the Saracens at Santiago, and St Thomas (**46**), the acts of the apostles are principally narrated in the central apsidal chapel, although almost half of this glass is late 19th-century, the original glass having been lost before the end of the 17th century. The lives of martyrs and confessors are intermingled on either side; within the south-east chapel, for example, are St Remy (**28**), St Nicholas (**27**), St Margaret and St Catherine (**26**) and St Thomas Becket (**25**), and in the north-east chapel, St Theodore and St Vincent (**39**), St Stephen (**41**) and St Cheron (**42**).

Between this north-east and the central apsidal chapels is the Charlemagne window (page 75), one of the finest in Chartres Cathedral.

Placed appropriately next to the famous 12th-century Notre-Dame de la Belle Verrière (The Blue Virgin, page 41) is an early 13th-century window,

BELOW: *Isachar, the high priest, rejects the sacrifice offered by Joachim and Anna (3).*

restored in 1993, which narrates Mary's life. It is inspired firstly from apocryphal texts that tell of her parents, her conception, childhood and betrothal to Joseph, followed by the biblical narrative from the Annunciation to the Flight into Egypt.

In the bottom corners are the donors: on the left (1) vintners pruning a vine and, on the right, (2) Thibault VI, Count of Chartres, on horseback with closed visor and a shield bearing the arms of the House of Champagne, of which the counts of Chartres were a younger branch. He is here probably endowing a monastery.

The apocryphal scenes in the bottom half of the window were doubtlessly inspired by the 'De Navitate Mariae', a Latin revision of the *Protevangelium* of James, which was well known in medieval Chartres, because it is referred to in the writings of Saint Fulbert (died 1028).

According to the *Protevangelium*, Anna and Joachim, Mary's parents, like Sarah and Abraham, had reached old age childless, and came to the temple in Jerusalem (3) to offer a sacrificial lamb, but the high priest, Isachar, dressed in brown and white, rejected their offering, proclaiming 'It is not fitting for you to offer your gifts, because you have begotten no offspring in Israel'. Anna, on the far right, in green, alarmed, with raised hand, makes to leave the temple. Joachim (4) 'was very sad . . . and betook himself into the wilderness and fasted 40 days and nights'. He is standing, alone, amongst his flock, with shepherd's crook, when an angel appeared, upper left, and announced that he would father a daughter to be named Mary, and that she would be the mother of the Messiah.

Meanwhile, Anna had returned home (5), and is here shown spinning, when an angel likewise appeared to her, saying, 'Anna, Anna, you shall conceive and bear and your offspring shall be spoken of in the whole world . . . Behold, Joachim, your husband is coming with his flocks.'

Between these scenes Anna greets Joachim at the Golden Gate of Jerusalem (6), saying 'Now I know that the Lord God has greatly blessed me . . . and I, who was childless, have conceived (shall conceive).' In 1854, the Vatican, in a papal bull, *Ineffabilis Deus*, proclaimed the Immaculate Conception as a dogma of faith, that 'the Blessed Virgin Mary, in the first instance of her conception, by a singular grace and privilege granted by Almighty God, in view of the merits of Jesus Christ, the saviour of the human race, was preserved from all stain of original sin.' In the next scene (7), Anna and Joachim are seated indoors beneath two arches. Joachim, having made his offerings at the temple 'went unto his house to await the fulfilment of the divine promise'.

'And her months were fulfilled, and in the ninth month Anna brought forth (8), and she said unto the midwife (standing behind in green with the infant in her arms, and gently touching the reclining Anna's shoulder): What have I brought forth? And she said: A female ... and when the days (forty) were fulfilled, Anna purified herself, and called her child Mary.'

In the adjacent panel, (9) two midwives are bathing the infant Mary in a curious red chalice-shaped tub.

The next two scenes concern Mary's education. As a child, dressed in yellow, she is first (10) taken to the temple by her parents to be instructed by a master, seated in green, birch in hand! Then (11) she is at school with other children, heads studiously bent over their books: the master is enthroned royally, a sceptre in his left hand.

The last apocryphal scenes narrate Mary's betrothal to Joseph. According to the *Protevangelium* (Chapters 8 and 9), 'When she was 12 years old there took place a council of priests', who decided that Mary should be wedded to a member of the House of David, 'and, lo, an angel of the Lord appeared saying: Go forth and assemble them that are widowers of the people, and let them bring every man a rod, and to whomsoever the Lord shall show a sign, his wife shall she be ... Joseph received the last rod, and behold a dove came out of the rod and flew onto Joseph's head.' There is no dove in the Chartres panel (12). Instead, Joseph's rod blossomed, whilst the others laid dry upon an altar. 'And the priest said: Joseph to you has fallen the good fortune to receive the virgin of the Lord.'

Hence (13) Mary, on the left, in brown, witnessed by two haloed figures, was betrothed to Joseph by the High Priest, apparelled in blue with a scarlet cape, and medieval papal-like tiara, his hand outstretched towards Joseph.

The upper half of this window concerns Mary's biblical role as the instrument of the Incarnation, as narrated in the central west 12th-century lancet window (see page 32).

First, Gabriel (14) announced to Mary, who has risen from her seat, that she will be god-bearer (*theotokos*). She then visited her cousin, Elizabeth (15), and they greet joyfully, having both conceived. A plant indicates that the scene takes place out-of-doors. In the nativity scene (16), as was customary in the 12th and 13th centuries, Mary reclines. Joseph is seated nearby, and the Child is placed sacrificially and sacramentally upon an altar, behind which are the traditional ox and the ass. An angel (17) swoops from a cloud to awaken two shepherds with their dog and surrounded by their sheep.

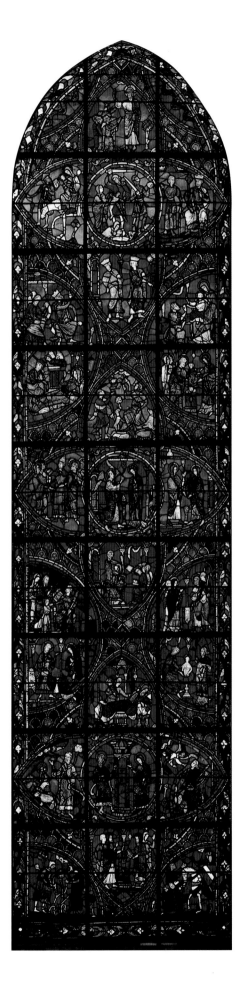

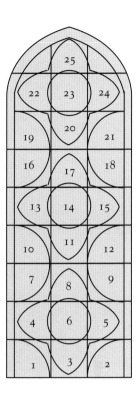

LEFT: *Life of Mary window, about 1212.*

In accordance with the Jewish law, 40 days after childbirth, Mary had to present her first-born son at the temple (18). Old Simeon is about to take Him up into his arms, and two women stand nearby, the one holding a candle (candlemass), and the other, probably the prophetess, Anne, is bringing gifts to the temple. To the left, (19) Herod is seated with scribes and priests consulting the Scriptures to discover where the Messiah should be born. Two of the magi (20), looking back towards Herod, are following the star to Bethlehem, whilst the third (21) is already offering his gift, and adoring the Christ Child, having removed his own crown in deference to the King of Kings.

The last three panels depict the massacre of the Holy Innocents and the Flight into Egypt. Herod, on the right (24) is seated, with a sceptre, ordering the massacre, shown violently in the central panel (23). Chain-mailed soldiers, armed with swords, snatch infants from their mothers. One of the assassins is holding the head of a child whose decapitated body lies upon the ground.

Meanwhile, the Holy Family fled into Egypt (22). Mary is seated upon a mule, led by Joseph, carrying a bundle across his shoulder and looking back concernedly towards mother and Child.

Jesus, standing, in the top panel (25) is blessing a group of kneeling people, very similar to those in the bottom right scene (2).

ABOVE: *Supervised by the schoolmaster on his throne, Mary and her fellows study their books (11).*

RIGHT: *Anna and Joachim greet one another at the Golden Gate of Jerusalem (6). Detail from the Life of Mary window.*

The Zodiac Signs Window

Like the adjacent Life of Mary, this early 13th-century window was also restored in 1993, and was donated, again, by vintners, carrying hoes in the tiny bottom corners (1 and 2), and pruning a vine in the bottom left circle (3). Opposite (4) is again Count Thibault VI of Chartres, bearing the same heraldry as in the Mary window, and once more being greeted by a group of kneeling people. Beneath his horse's hooves is a Latin inscription, very difficult to decipher, because of earlier restorations, but which suggests that the window was donated by Thibault on behalf of Thomas, a count of Perche. Between these two signatures is another curious scene which takes place beneath an arch (5) probably inside a church. A bent figure is pulling upon a rope, perhaps bell-ringing, whilst two others (6), holding sticks, stand by watching.

The rest of this window should be read bottom upwards, with the Zodiac signs in the right half, including the central quatrefoils, and the corresponding monthly labours in the left half, the whole representing a calendar, the cycle of a year.

The Roman deity Janus (7), origin of the word January, is not feasting at a table, as on the Royal Portal and elsewhere, but is standing, opening doors that represent the new year. Janus is usually represented two-faced, the one aged, the other youthful, again suggesting the cycle of time. The Janus shown here is a rarer example of a triple-faced figure: time being composed of a past, present and future. He shares the quatrefoil with Aquarius (8) dressed in red and pouring water from a yellow pot.

Warmly clothed and hooded, February (9) is seated by a roaring fire toasting his hands and feet. Beside him is a jug of wine and a poker. Opposite (10), Pisces is represented in the usual way: two fish, head-to-tail, their mouths linked by a cord. March (11) is a hooded peasant pruning his vine. Opposite (12), is Aries, a ram standing amongst trees.

The months of April and May are inverted, so that, in the next central quatrefoil, are May (15) and Gemini (16). May is portrayed as a helmeted soldier, wearing chain-mail, carrying a shield and holding a banner, whilst his saddled horse grazes near him. Gemini, the Twins, in the same panel, are naked, and hold hands.

April (13), the month when nature is reborn, is personified by a woman standing between flowering trees, holding a bouquet of flowers in each hand.

Taurus, the Bull (14), like Aries, stands amongst trees. June (17) is mowing with a blue scythe. The inscription is JULIUS, although it is not certain whether this is an original mistake or that of a later restorer. Cancer (18) is a red crab-like creature. July (19) again has a mistaken inscription, JUNIUS, and is represented by a peasant cutting wheat with a

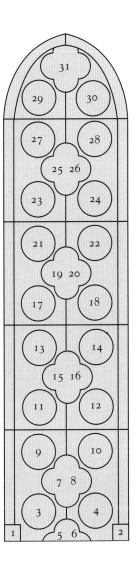

LEFT: *The Zodiac Signs window, early 13th century.*

sickle. He shares the third quatrefoil with Leo (20), the Lion.

August (21) is stripped to the waist and, with a flail, is threshing wheat. Various farming instruments are stacked to either side of him. Virgo (22), like April, holds flowers in each hand. September (23) is portrayed as two vintners cutting bunches of grapes off a vine, and treading them in a vat. Libra (24) is represented by a woman holding a pair of scales.

In the next quatrefoil, October (25) sits astride a barrel into which he is pouring new wine, and Scorpio (26) is shown as a green creature, with a twisted sting-tipped tail.

November (27), although the inscription is DECEMBER is about to stun a pig with the back of an axe. Sagittarius (28) is a centaur, half man half beast, holding a bow in one hand, and arrows in the other. December (29) is feasting at a table on which are three Christian symbols, bread, wine and fish as on the Last Supper table (page 37), and Capricorn (30) is half goat and half fish, the fish being a symbol for Jesus, whose advent is feasted in the sign of Capricorn. He (31), as Chronocrator, is enthroned in the uppermost panel. He is seated between two candles, and the Greek letters alpha and omega. Time, hence, is both linear and cyclic.

ABOVE: *A curious, crab-like representation of Cancer (18). Detail from the Zodiac Signs window.*

RIGHT: *Wrapped in a cloak and with wine jug and poker near at hand, February warms his hands and bare feet before a roaring fire (9).*

OPPOSITE: *The Zodiac Signs Window, from August/Virgo to November/Sagittarius (21–28). November is incorrectly inscribed as December.*

DECENBER

SAGITARIVS

OCTOBER SCORPIO

SEPTENBER

LIBRA

VIRGO

AVGVSTVS

IVNIVS LEO

THE CHARLEMAGNE WINDOW

Dating from the early 13th century, this window was donated by furriers, like the St Eustace window, for Charlemagne, like St Eustace, was a hunter. At the base of the window a furrier (1) displays a fur coat to a long-sleeved aristocratic customer.

Although not recognized by the Church as a saint, Charlemagne was canonized in 1165 by the anti-Pope Pascal III upon the request of Frederick Barbarossa, who also commissioned the writing of a book narrating Charlemagne's deeds and merits and which contained the texts of the *Journey to Jerusalem* and the *Pseudo-Turpin Chronicle*, the sources which inspired both this and a similar window, destroyed during the French Revolution, at the royal abbey of Saint-Denis.

2–7 The Journey to Jerusalem

It was probably an 11th-century monk at Saint-Denis who wrote the chronicle of Charlemagne's legendary crusade to Jerusalem, undoubtedly in an attempt to authenticate the relics of Christ's Passion given to the royal abbey by Charlemagne's grandson, Charles the Bald. The lower third of the Chartres window illustrates this text. In the first scene (2) Charlemagne, crowned and with a green nimbus, is seated beneath a cusped arch, speaking with two bishops, one of whom, to the left, could be Turpin, Archbishop of Reims, summoned to interpret a letter brought by the other, a Byzantine bishop, from Constantine VI, telling of his vision.

In this vision (3), an angel, upper left, revealed to him as he slept that Charlemagne would deliver Jerusalem from the infidels. In contrast to the reclining Constantine, Charlemagne is portrayed very upright astride a horse, wearing coat of mail, spurs and a helmet with closed visor, carrying a red shield and oriflammed lance. He is similarly attired in the following scene (4), which represents the Battle of Jerusalem, but wears a red mantle over his armour as he strikes a fatal blow at the neck of a fleeing Saracen king. Throughout this window the Christians have flat-topped shields and helmets, whereas the Saracens carry circular shields and have conical helmets.

On his victorious return from the Holy Land, Charlemagne visits Constantine (5), who welcomes him at the gate of Constantinople. The beardless figure accompanying Charlemagne could be his youthful nephew, Roland. In order to thank him for his triumph over the infidels, Constantine (6), shown standing on the right, rewarded Charlemagne not with riches but, at his request, with sacred relics including fragments of the crown of thorns and the cross, the shroud of Christ, Mary's Sancta Camisia and the arm upon which Simeon

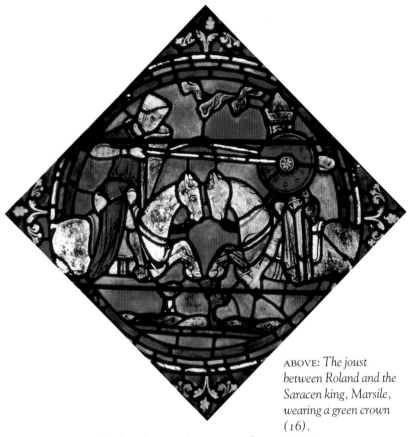

ABOVE: *The joust between Roland and the Saracen king, Marsile, wearing a green crown (16).*

held the Christ Child at the temple, contained in the ornate reliquaries set upon an altar.

In the final scene (7) taken from the *Journey to Jerusalem*, Charlemagne kneels before the altar at Aix-la-Chapelle Cathedral, offering a reliquary in the form of a crown which probably encloses the fragment of the crown of thorns. Above the altar and incorporated into the architecture are three more reliquaries, perhaps containing the other relics brought back from Constantinople. The youthful figure standing behind Charlemagne could again be Roland. Above Charlemagne and hanging beneath an arch is a horn, similar to the oliphant sounded by Roland in panel 19.

8–21 The Pseudo-Turpin Chronicle

A variant of the better-known *Song of Roland*, the *Pseudo-Turpin Chronicle* was wrongly attributed to Turpin, Archbishop of Reims. In fact it was the work of several anonymous authors who, during the 11th and 12th centuries, popularized the epic story of Charlemagne's three expeditions to Spain and his conflicts there with the infidels.

The narrative begins (8) with a discussion between Charlemagne, seated and crowned and with a red halo, and two other figures. The central one, wearing a skull-cap, is probably a philosopher at the imperial court. He is pointing towards the Milky Way, shown as an undulating cloud over their

OPPOSITE: *The Ambulatory, with steps leading to the St Piat Chapel and cathedral treasury. Mary's relic is now on permanent display in the chapel on the left.*

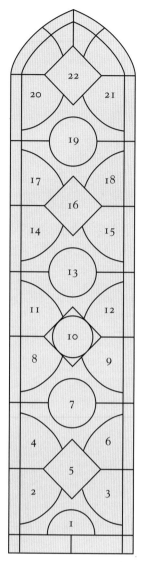

heads, and Charlemagne wonders where it might lead. As Charlemagne sleeps (9), St James the Greater appears to him in a dream, and explains that the Milky Way leads to his desecrated tomb in Galicia, which he wishes Charlemagne to deliver from the infidels. Charlemagne then sets out on horseback upon the first Spanish crusade (10). Again crowned, he is the central figure amongst five others, also mounted. The bishop on the right is Turpin, and the youth leading is Roland.

When his army arrives in Spain (11), the soldiers dressed in chain mail, helmeted and with standards flying aloft from lances, Charlemagne, in a curious half-kneeling position, prays for victory and that the walls of Pamplona may collapse. The *Pseudo-Turpin Chronicle* lists cities taken after Pamplona, some by consent, others by force, and the next scene (12) probably generalizes all the Spanish cities that fell and is not specifically Pamplona, whose walls are usually shown crumbling. A figure upon the ramparts sounds the alarm by blowing a horn, whilst a Christian warrior pursues a fleeing Saracen through the city gate.

According to the Pseudo-Turpin, Charlemagne's second journey to Spain began with the construction of a church to honour St Facundus and St Primitivus. This church assumed considerable importance during the 11th and 12th centuries and several members of the House of Aragon were buried there. It ruled over nearly a hundred monasteries, and was the principal centre of French Cluniac influence in Spain. It is perhaps the con-

struction of this church (13), with anachronistic flying buttresses and masons carrying stone up a meshed ladder, which Charlemagne, on horseback, is here ordering with raised hand.

Next (14) comes another battle scene, in which a Christian soldier, in the left foreground, is slaying a Saracen whilst another Saracen flees. This panel probably illustrates a passage in the Pseudo-Turpin text which states that Saracen warriors were either killed or put to flight, and does not represent any specific battle. Similarly, the soldiers in panel 15, whose lances flowered while they slept as a sign that they were the 'certain from among the Christians' destined for martyrdom in battle, are not, in the text, identified individually.

Charlemagne's third journey to Spain is depicted in the next six panels, and begins (16) with a joust between Roland, shown on the left with closed visor, and the Saracen king, Marsile, wearing a green crown. He is depicted astride a reddish horse and carrying a circular shield, illustrating the Pseudo-Turpin text, 'Marsirum cum equo rubeo et clipeo rotundo'. Marsile's lance is breaking against Roland's shield, then (17), having been felled from his horse but still crowned, he is killed through his navel. The text does not, in fact, describe King Marsile's death and the killing through the navel refers to the way in which Roland slew Ferragut, for it was only here that he was vulnerable. Ferragut was a Saracen giant, but was not royal. Perhaps this scene is intended to combine Roland's killing of both Marsile and Ferragut!

Charlemagne, crowned and with a red nimbus, is next seen (18) riding through mountainous country, accompanied by Turpin (?) on the left, wearing not a mitre but a skull-cap and by Ganelon, whose treachery caused the death of Roland as he was bringing up the rear-guard after the Battle of Roncevaux (see below).

During the 13th century it was generally accepted that Roland was a saint, and he is depicted twice in the following panel (19) with a red nimbus. Having fought a fierce rear-guard battle, attested by the slain Saracens strewn about him, and although mortally wounded, he tries to destroy his sword, Durendal, against a rock, but only cleaves the rock in two. In the right half of the same panel, he is blowing his oliphant, the sound of which was carried to Charlemagne by an angel. Baldwin (20), having been unable to find water for his dying half-brother, Roland, seen propped against his shield, shows him his empty helmet and then (21) catches up with Charlemagne to tell him of Roland's death.

The final panel (22), in the apex of the window, depicts the Mass of St Giles, intended for the forgiveness of Charlemagne's terrible sin, which he

dared not even confess. In the 13th century the sin was made explicit as an incestuous relationship with his sister, from which it has been suggested that Roland was born. Charlemagne is seated on the left, thoughtfully, chin in hand, whilst the hermit St Giles, accompanied by a deacon holding a book, celebrates Mass. Above the altar hovers an angel, dangling a parchment upon which the unconfessed sin is written.

The window was last restored in 1921 and the panels placed in the present order. Originally, however, the Mass of St Giles was in the position of panel 16, and the apex scene was the joust between Roland and King Marsile. It has recently been argued (Clark Maines: 'The Charlemagne window at Chartres: new considerations on text and image', *Speculum* 52 (October 1977), 801–23), that by altering the original order the restorers destroyed a former typological meaning in which Marsile personified the infidels and Roland the Church militant, for in the early 13th century, when this window was made, Christians would have been very aware that the Crusaders were still fighting to deliver the Holy Land from the Saracens.

ABOVE: *Roland is shown twice here (19), attempting to break his sword on the left and blowing his horn on the right. Detail from the Charlemagne window.*

77

THE PARABLE OF THE PRODIGAL SON WINDOW

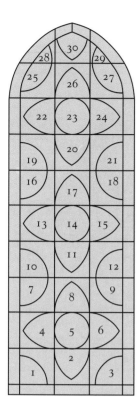

RIGHT: *The Prodigal Son window, about 1210.*

The narrative of this window closely follows the text of Luke 15:32, with, as in a similar window at Bourges Cathedral, extra scenes to illustrate the youth's 'riotous living'.

'A certain man had two sons; and the younger of them said to his father, "Father, give me the portion of goods that falleth to me".' The father is seated (1) in green, wearing a skull-cap, then stands (2) beside an open yellow chest, and gives his son a golden goblet and a handful of coins, whilst the older son (3), in the fields tending cattle, looks enviously back towards the family scene.

'And not many days later, the younger son gathered all together, and took his journey into a far country.' He sets out (4) upon a horse, led by a servant, with a small white dog sitting upright behind him on the horse's rump.

The following scenes (5–15) illustrate Luke 15:13. 'And he wasted his substance in riotous living.' Two harlots await him as he arrives at a city. His servant, dressed in blue, disapproving, appears to abandon his master (5 and 6). The prodigal wines and dines the two women sumptuously (8), the one in green kissing him, whilst servants to either side (7 and 9) bring one lavish dish after another from the kitchens to the table.

After another kissing and cuddling session (11) in which one of the women crowns him with flowers, he is awakened by two people (10). He is sitting up in bed, his arm around the waist of the woman in green, whom he appears to recognize, but with her is a man, dressed in yellow, pointing to the right, where (12) he then sits at a chequered board with an adversary throwing dice. He has been enticed to gamble, and loses all.

Next (13) two youths and a woman, possibly his debtors, beat him and strip him to his breeches. His shirt is pulled over his head, so that in the next scenes he is reduced to begging, half-naked, from women, perhaps the harlots, who admonish him (14), and threaten him with a stick (15).

'There arose a mighty famine in the land; and he began to be in want. And he went and joined himself to a citizen of that country.' They are here seen (16) shaking hands upon an agreement they have made. 'And he sent him into his fields to feed swine.' Now wearing a peasant's smock (17) the prodigal knocks down acorns to feed the pigs then (18), huddled amongst them, 'he came to himself and said, "How many hired servants of my father's have bread enough and to spare, and I perish with hunger! I will arise and go to my father".'

No longer the carefree horseman who left home, he returns on foot (19), humbly clad in peasant's smock, carrying a swineherd's scrip and baton. When his father greets him warmly (20), he 'said unto him, "Father, I have sinned against Heaven, and in thy sight, and am no more worthy to be called thy son".'

'But the father said to his servants, "Bring forth the best robe (21) and put it on him . . . and bring forth the fatted calf, and kill it (22) and let us eat and be merry".' Cooks busy themselves (23) around a huge kitchen pot, suspended over a fire, whilst a child, in blue, turns meat upon a spit.

'Now his elder son . . . came and drew nigh to the house (24) . . . and was angry and would not go in: therefore came his father out and intreated him.' In the remaining narrative scenes the father reconciles his two sons at a banquet (26) with musicians on the left (25) playing a rebeck and tapping upon a tambourine, whilst servants on the right (27) bring more food and wine to the table.

In the apex of this window, two angels (28 and 29) adore Christ (30) blessing the world.

According to early Christian exegetes, the

LEFT: *A lavish feast is provided for the harlots at the errant son's expense (8).*

LEFT: *The prodigal son, stripped to the waist, gambling at a chequered board (12). His adversary holds three dice. Detail from the Prodigal Son window. North transept.*

79

BELOW: *Reduced to poverty, the prodigal son begs from a woman (14).*

PRO DI FILIO

RIGHT: *The St Gervais and St Protais window in the south arm of the transept, east wall, was perhaps given by a priest named Geoffrey, shown standing at an altar.*

CENTRE: *One of the south nave clerestory lancets, representing a standing Virgin, one breast uncovered, about to suckle the Christ Child upon her arm. Beneath her is a 'Noli me tangere' scene.*

father in the parable represents God, the Father. The elder son personifies the Jews, and the younger son, the Gentiles.

The remaining ambulatory windows narrate more lives of martyrs and confessors, too numerous to describe in the present text. The exceptions to this vast hagiography are, first, the grisaille windows, from differing periods, usually added to give more light. Secondly, there are four modern windows in the transept, the original glass in this case having been destroyed in 1791 to light up Baroque altars, since demolished. All four are the work of François Lorin: the St Fulbert window (**12**),

donated by the American Architects' Association in 1954; the Peace window (**56**), which was given by the German Friends of Chartres Association in 1971; the two windows opposite (**57, 11**), although modern, contain fragments of medieval glass. Thirdly, an original early 13th-century window which appears unrelated iconographically to the other transept and ambulatory windows: the Zodiac window (page 71), in which the signs on the right correspond with the monthly labours on the left. Christ Chronocrator, in the apex, is seated between the Greek letters alpha and omega, for He was present at the beginning and at the end.

THE UPPER STOREY WINDOWS

Unlike the lower storey windows which are largely narrative, the upper ones contain for the most part only one, two, three or four figures or scenes in order to be seen from the ground. Except for the central group over the choir, they do not appear to form any particular iconographic programme. Mary and Child are given the place of honour, in the central apsidal lancet (**120**), high above the choir, visible from the whole length of the cathedral, with beneath them a Visitation and Annunciation, and the donors, bakers, carrying a basket of bread. Aaron (**121**), to the left, and Isaiah (**119**), to the right, both hold a flowering rod, symbol of the virgin birth. Beneath Isaiah is Moses and the burning bush which, enflamed but unconsumed, is yet another symbol for the virgin birth of Christ. The other three major prophets are in the two windows on either side: Daniel and Jeremiah (**118**), and David above Ezekiel (**122**). David, with crown and sceptre, the son of Jesse, is the ancestor of Mary and a prefiguration of her Son, a new king of the Jews.

BELOW RIGHT: *One of the choir lancets, representing two groups of peasant pilgrims. It was given by Robert de Bérou, a chancellor of the cathedral.*

THE SOUTH PORCH

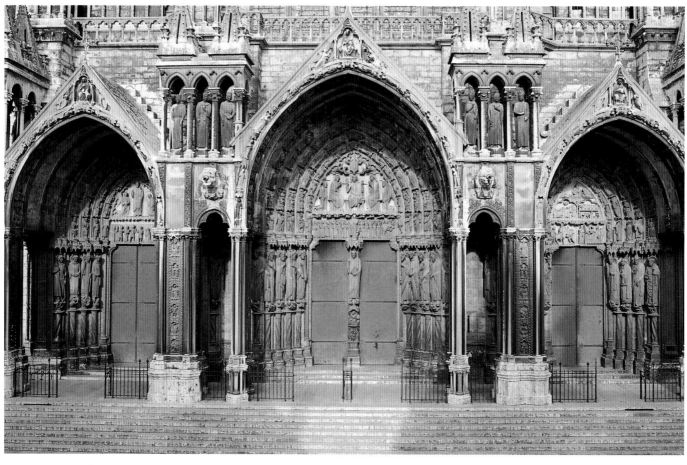

ABOVE: *The South Porch,*
early 13th century.

In the South Porch, Christ is triumphant with His Church both on Earth and in Heaven. He is the central trumeau figure, the Word made flesh, bare-footed and trampling upon the lion and dragon, symbolizing (Ps. 91:13) the crushing of the forces of evil. To either side stand His twelve apostles. To His left Paul is traditionally portrayed bald and John beardless, a cup of poison upon the pedestal referring to one of his apocryphal miracles. James the Greater with his attribute, shells, is followed by James the Less with a club, Bartholomew with a knife (broken) and Matthew with his Gospel, like John. To Christ's right Peter, with keys, carries a cross, as does Andrew; the remaining four carry swords, the instruments of their martyrdom, and must be Simon, Jude, Philip and Thomas, although it is not possible to identify them individually. Like Christ they are bare-footed and triumph over their persecutors, for the most part Roman emperors, sculpted on the pedestals.

In the left bay, on Christ's right, stand the martyrs who died for Him, likewise triumphing over their martyrdom. The outer figures are St George to the right, his death upon the wheel depicted on the pedestal, and to the left another military saint, with a king worshipping an idol on the pedestal and with fleur-de-lis upon his shield. He has been variously

named as St Theodore, St Maurice (in which cases the shield heraldry and the pedestal figure are difficult to explain) or Roland. The other figures form two groups of three: on both sides two deacons holding books, St Stephen and St Lawrence to the left and St Vincent and St Piat to the right, flank a pope, on the left St Clement and on the right St Denis or perhaps St Ignatius of Antioch, who was thrown to the lions in Rome. On the lintel is the stoning of Stephen, and in the tympanum the supreme martyr, Christ Himself.

In the right bay, on Christ's left, are the confessors, those who best exemplified His teaching: Nicholas and Martin, the innermost figures, with their acts of charity sculpted on the lintel over the door; then facing each other two doctors of the Church, St Ambrose of Milan to the left and an ascetic, the gentle St Jerome, to the right, pointing to his translation of the Bible. Next come two popes, St Silvester, perhaps, on the left and St Gregory on the right, inspired to reform the Church by the Holy Spirit, perched upon his shoulder. The outer figures, St Laumer on the left and St Avitus on the right, local saints, were later additions and are in a different style, with heavier drapery folds.

The sculptural programme culminates in the central bay, with the Last Judgement. Christ is seated

PRECEDING PAGES:
Chartres Cathedral
from the north-east.

LEFT: *The central tympanum of the South Porch, representing the Last Judgement. Christ the Judge is the central figure, showing His wounds. Mary on His right and John the Divine on His left intercede for humanity with joined hands. Angels above and on either side carry the instruments of Christ's Passion. Beneath Christ's feet is St Michael, holding scales, while the damned, on his left hand, go in procession to Hell, shown as an open mouth, and the saved, on his right, are led by an angel to Paradise.*

ABOVE: *A lion sculpted on the pedestal of a statue thought to represent St Denis or St Ignatius of Antioch, who was thrown to the lions.*

in the tympanum, showing His earthly wounds, with angels to the extreme left and right and above, carrying the instruments of His Passion. Seated beside Him, equal in size, and not kneeling as in most other representations elsewhere, are Mary to His right and John the Divine to His left, hands joined, pleading as intercessors for humanity. Four angels in the outer archivolt blow trumpets and the celestial court is assembled: seraphim, cherubim and thrones; dominations, virtues and powers; prince-doms, archangels and angels. Those to be judged – all humanity – in the second row across the archi-volts, climb from their tombs and await the sen-tence, carried out upon the lintel, where St Michael holds scales (broken).

To his and Christ's left is the procession of the damned, their fingers turned downwards. Demons hurl them into the open jaws of Hell. To the right of St Michael is the procession of those judged worthy of regaining Paradise, fingers turned up-wards. Their resurrected flesh may be reunited with the soul and rocked in the bosom of Abraham, a symbol for Paradise. At the base of the three outer archivolts on the extreme left, crowned by angels with the crown of life, triumphant over time and death, they enter the Heavenly Jerusalem to begin an eternal life.

LEFT: *Abraham with the blessed in his bosom, a symbol for Paradise. South Porch, central bay.*

ABOVE: *Pride falling from his horse. South Porch, left bay, right pier, south face.*

BELOW: *The martyrdom of St Thomas Becket, whose friend and secretary, John of Salisbury, became one of the most illustrious bishops of Chartres. South Porch, left bay.*

RIGHT: *Figures from the right jamb of the central bay of the South Porch. From left to right, the apostles Paul, John, James the Greater, James the Less and Bartholomew.*

THE WEST ROSE WINDOW

Christ's second coming as judge is also the subject of the West Rose window (about 1215) (**176**), appropriately placed above the three 12th-century lancets which narrate His first coming, and facing west, as was frequently the case in medieval churches, so that the sun sets upon the evening of time.

Christ the Judge is seated in the centre of the window, displaying His five bleeding wounds. He is surrounded by three series of twelve circles. The inner series, set in the tips of the elliptical forms, contain eight angels, placed in pairs between the four apocalyptic animals, representing the four evangelists, at the cardinal points. The eagle above Christ's head symbolizes St John, the winged man beneath His feet St Matthew, the lion on His right hand St Mark, and the ox on His left St Luke. In the series of larger circles, also contained within the ellipses, are Christ's twelve apostles, seated in pairs, helping Him judge the twelve tribes. Above Christ, Abraham rocks souls in his bosom, flanked by cherubim with multiple wings. Above them, in the

BELOW: *The West Rose window, representing the Last Judgement, 1215.*

outer circles, angels carry the instruments of Christ's Passion. Then, still in the outer circles, follow identical scenes on either side: angels blowing trumpets to announce the Day of Judgement and, beneath them, the shroud-clad resurrected who, in six scenes, having climbed from their tombs, await to be judged. Beneath Christ's feet, in the central circles, St Michael, with scales, and a demon, representing the conflicting forces of good and evil, weigh up at the end of time the deeds of those being judged. To the right of St Michael a fierce red-faced demon with a long fork prods the damned towards Hell which, in the outer bottom left circle, is shown as in the South Porch as a gaping mouth with teeth, eyes and a snout. A miser, his money-bag around his neck, languishes in the midst of the flames. Beside this scene (on the right) more demons lift and hurl the damned into Hell while above them, to the left of St Michael, an angel leads the elect, crowned with the crown of life, towards Paradise Regained.

ABOVE: *Abraham (in the centre) rocking the souls of the blessed in his bosom. Detail from the West Rose window.*

LEFT: *St Michael and a demon weigh up the deeds of a soul. Detail from the West Rose window.*

THE SOUTH ROSE WINDOW

This remarkable ensemble (about 1225) may be considered as a synthesis of the complete Chartres iconographic text. The donor, Pierre Mauclerc, was Count of Dreux and, through his marriage, Duke of Brittany. His heraldry is placed at the base of the central lancet, chequered blue and gold for Dreux and ermine for Brittany. The family is portrayed on either side at the base of the other four lancets: Pierre to the right, kneeling, with his son John standing on the far right; whilst his wife, Alix de Thouars, kneels to the left and his daughter Yolande stands on the far left.

In the central lancet Mary, crowned, with her Child upon her left arm, stands between the four major prophets of the Old Testament carrying astride their shoulders the four New Testament evangelists, thus brilliantly demonstrating the concordance of the two testaments and the belief that Mary was the instrument whereby the Old Testament prophecies were accomplished and the New brought through her Son.

On either side of her, from left to right, Jeremiah carries St Luke, Isaiah carries St Matthew, Ezekiel carries St John and Daniel carries St Mark. Like dwarfs upon the shoulders of giants, the evangelists are smaller yet see further, but only because the prophets have lifted them up. The Old Testament prepared for the New; the New is built upon the Old. 'Think not that I am come to destroy the law, or the prophets', said Jesus, 'I am not come to destroy but to fulfil' (Matt. 5:17).

The two testaments thus form the law by which humanity will be judged at the end of time and through which the saved may achieve eternal life in the Heavenly Jerusalem. It is this city which is represented, as described in the Book of the Revelation, in the rose window above.

In the centre of the rose is Christ as the apocalyptic One, seated upon an emerald throne. Immediately surrounding Him are eight censing angels in pairs, and between them the four symbols for the four evangelists – man, eagle, ox and lion – in their turn surrounded in the circles and semicircles by the twenty-four elders of the Apocalypse, holding a variety of musical instruments in their left hands, and in their right 'golden vials full of odours, which are the prayers of saints', and, as on the Royal Portal, giving 'glory and honour and thanks to him that sat on the throne, who liveth for ever and ever'.

TOP: *Detail from the South Rose window, showing elders of the Apocalypse holding medieval musical instruments in one hand and vases containing the perfume of the prayers of the saints in the other.*

OPPOSITE: *The South Rose window and lancets. About 1225.*

RIGHT: *Jeremiah carrying St Luke. Detail from the lancets of the South Rose window.*

The masterbuilders and theologians who conceived and constructed Chartres Cathedral, and her sisters, were inspired by various Biblical sources, which included the descriptions of Noah's ark and the Temple of Solomon, both symbols for Christ's Church – the ark as a means of salvation, the temple because it was built by Solomon who prefigured Christ in His wisdom and as judge.

The principal inspiration, however, came from apocalyptic visions of a heavenly city in both the Old and New Testaments:

'O thou afflicted, tossed with tempest, and not comforted, behold, I will lay thy stones with fair colours, and lay their foundation with sapphires. And I will make thy windows of agates, and thy gates of carbuncles, and all thy borders of pleasant stones' (Isaiah 54:11–12).

But the greatest inspiration of all was the Book of the Revelation, in which the author saw and described 'The holy city, New Jerusalem coming down from God, out of Heaven, prepared as a bride adorned for her husband . . . and her light was like unto a stone most precious . . . and the building of the wall of it was jasper, and the city was pure gold, like unto clear glass. And the foundations of the wall of the city were garnished with all manner of precious stones' (12 in all like the 12 tribes of Israel), 'jasper, sapphire, chalcedony, emerald, sardonyx, sardonius, chrysolite, beryl, topaz, chrysoprasus, jacinth and amethyst' (Rev. 21 especially verses 18–20).

The people of the Middle Ages knew that their cathedral-church was the seat (cathedra) of their bishop, but that, above all, it was a symbol within their city for the Heavenly Jerusalem, dwarfing all else, including the count's castle. Built inside a close where, at Chartres, some 600 people lived – canons, priests and their servants – it formed a spiritual city within the city, as the Vatican does in Rome, and outside the jurisdiction of the count, which is why sanctuary could be sought within the close. Like an embassy today, which is our territory within another land, and where we may seek refuge, so in medieval times a cathedral was one of God's embassies; the bishop being, as it were, a celestial ambassador.

For the medieval pilgrim, drawn by the cathedral steeples, like beacons, beckoning from afar, the cathedral awaiting them at the end of their journey would similarly be a symbol for the Heavenly Jerusalem awaiting his soul at the end of its journey.

This impression would be strengthened by the nine entrances, with their thousands of sculptures, at that time polychromed, painted, gilded and with many inscriptions. The canopies over their heads, in fact, symbolize the New Jerusalem. Awestruck, the pilgrim would pass, as it were, through the gates of Paradise into the heavenly city itself, with its walls opened up and set with glittering jewel-like stained-glass windows which diffuse a mystic and divine essence: light.

OPPOSITE: *A watch-tower on the medieval city ramparts overlooks the River Eure.*

BELOW: *Jesus, Redeemer, blessing, seated between two triple-branched candlesticks. Apex of the Redemption window.*

'And God shall wipe away all tears from their eyes, and there shall be no more death, neither sorrow, nor crying, neither shall there be any more pain: for the former things are passed away' (Rev. 21:4), leaving only Peace.

In both the stained glass and the sculpture of Chartres Cathedral objects and animals are used to symbolize the Trinity, God the Father, God the Son and God the Holy Ghost, or to identify particular people or to draw attention to particular ideas or significant relationships between people or events. In this glossary the most important of these symbols are given with a brief explanation and a reference to the window panel as shown in the detailed diagram in the text, or the window itself (with the number on the plan on pp 4/5 in brackets) or group of sculptures in which an example can be seen, and the page of this book on which it is discussed.

Abraham Prefigures God the Father in relationship to the Son, Isaac/Christ. *Redemption window 20, p 51; North Porch, p 45.*

Altar In the account of the Nativity, the crib may be shown as an altar, symbolizing both sacrifice and the presence in the Eucharist. *Incarnation window 3, p 32; Life of Mary window 16, p 69, Royal Portal, p 28.*

Apple Symbol for the forbidden fruit because of the Latin word *malum* which means both apple and evil. *Good Samaritan window 16, p 64; North Porch, p 44.*

Assumption The doctrine whereby Mary's body was assumed into heaven on the third day after her death. *Assumption window 19, p 67; North Porch, p 45.*

Bald man In Old Testament context, the prophet Elijah. *Redemption window 24, p 52.* Amongst the Apostles, St Paul. *South Porch, p 84.*

Beardless man Amongst the Apostles, St John. *South Porch, p 85.*

Burning bush As seen by Moses in the Old Testament. Represents the unconsumed virginity of Mary in the context of the New Testament. *North Porch, p 47; Isaiah window (**119**), p 81.*

Cap, conical shape Denotes a Jew, particularly used to contrast with a Gentile. *Joseph window 1 and 2, p 54; Prodigal Son window 1, p 78.*

Club Amongst the Apostles, James the Less. *South Porch, p 84.*

Cross, green The Cross on which Christ was crucified is sometimes shown in the colour green, symbolic of the life-giving power of the blood of the Lord and a reference to the belief that the Cross was made of the wood of the Tree of Life from the Garden of Eden. *Passion and Resurrection window 7, p 38; Redemption window 5 and 20, pp 50/51; Small rose (**18**) above the Zodiac Signs window (**17**).*

Dove The Holy Spirit. *Incarnation window 21, p 36; Assumption window 27, p 67.* Peace. *Noah window, 24, 25, p 56; St Gregory, South Porch, p 84.*

Dragon Symbol of Satanic forces. *North Porch, p 45; South Porch, p 84; Redemption Window 16, p 51.*

Eagle Amongst the Evangelists, St John. *West Rose window, p 88; South Rose, p 90.*

Ephod A pectoral with 12 precious stones. When worn by a Jewish priest, the stones denote the 12 tribes of Israel. *North Rose, Aaron, p 49.* When transferred to St Peter, they represent the 12 apostles. *North Porch, p 46.*

Fish Symbol of Christ. *Passion and Resurrection window 3, p 37.* Also refers to the miracle of the loaves and fishes. *Zodiac Signs window 29, p 72; Apostles window (**34**).*

Forty The number of purification. *Incarnation window 11, p 34; Noah window 29, p 56.*

Grapes on a pole Christ on the Cross. *Redemption window 8, p 50.*

Halo or nimbus, when cruciform, Christ or God the Father. *Numerous examples,* including *North Porch; Noah window 37, p 57; Passion window 3 and 4, pp 37/38.*

Horns Moses is shown with horns, the result of a mistranslation of the Hebrew into Latin. *Redemption window 16, p 51.* Not to be confused with the horns on demons.

Immaculate Conception The doctrine whereby Anne and Joachim conceived Mary, so that Mary, being immaculate, may, through a virgin conception, be mother of God incarnate. *Life of Mary window 6, p 68.*

Isaac Prefigures Christ, the sacrifice. *Redemption window 20, p 51; North Porch, p 45.*

Keys Amongst the Apostles, St Peter. *North Porch, p 47; South Porch, p 84.*

Lamb Symbol of Christ as the sacrifice. *North Porch, p 45; Redemption window 17 and 21, p 51.*

Lion Amongst the Evangelists, St Mark. *West Rose window, p 88.* In another context, the power of evil. *South Porch, p 84; Redemption window 28, p 52.*

Man, winged Amongst the Evangelists, St Matthew. *West Rose window, p 88; South Rose Window, p 90.*

Moon Symbol of the Old Testament. *Incarnation window, 25–30, p 36.*

Olive branch Peace. *Noah window 25, p 56; South Porch, concord amongst the virtues and vices, p 85.*

Ox Amongst the Evangelists, St Luke. *West Rose window, p 88; Royal Portal, p 28.*

Palm branch Symbol both of peace and of victory. *Incarnation window 22–24, p 36.*

Pelican Believed to resurrect its offspring with its own blood, and thus symbolic of both Jesus's sacrifice and the eucharist. *Redemption window 22, p 51/52.*

Ram in thicket In the account of Abraham and Isaac, symbol of Christ as the sacrifice. *North Porch, p 45; Redemption window 21, p 51.*

Rod, flowering Symbol of virgin birth. *Life of Mary window 12, p 69; Aaron and Isaiah windows, p 81; North Porch, p 45.*

Scales Symbol for justice held by St Michael in the Last Judgement. *South Porch, p 85; West Rose window, p 89.*

Sceptre Symbol of kingship; e.g. Herod. *Life of Mary window 24, p 70; Joseph window 22, p 55.*

Sceptre, herald's The sceptre of the classical messenger, Mercury, indicates the role of the Archangel Gabriel as the bringer of news. *Incarnation window 1, p 32.*

Serpent, 1 Evil in the creation story. *North Porch, p 44; Good Samaritan window 16, p 64.* **2** Wisdom. *South Porch, amongst the virtues and vices, p 85.* **3** The brazen serpent raised by Moses symbolizes the crucifixion. *North Porch, p 45; Redemption window 16, p 51.*

Seven The number that is the sum of three and four and the number of days in a week. Three, the first indivisible number after the number one, represents things spiritual and eternal, the Trinity. Four is the number of the elements (earth, air, fire and water) and thus stands for things temporal, of the material world. The sum represents the completeness of the spiritual and the temporal. *Jesse Window, the seven gifts of the Holy Spirit, p 31; Royal Portal, the liberal arts, p 28.*

Shells Amongst the Apostles, James the Greater. *South Porch, p 84.*

Sun The New Testament. *Incarnation window 25–30, p 36.*

Tree The Tree of Jesse symbolizes the descent of Christ from Jesse as prophesied by Isaiah. *Tree of Jesse window, pp 30/31.*

Twelve The number that is the product of three multiplied by four and thus another symbol of the completeness of things spiritual and temporal (see **Seven** above). There are 12 months in the year. *Joseph window 5, the brothers, representing the 12 tribes of Israel, p 54; North Rose and North Porch, see **Ephod** above; Zodiac Signs window, p 71; North Porch, the monthly labours, pp 46/47.*

Index